Emotional Self-Care

for Black Women

A Powerful Mental Health Workbook to
Silence Your Inner Critic, Raise Your
Self-Esteem, and Heal Yourself

Layla Moon

Emotional Self-Care for Black Women

PUBLISHED BY: Layla Moon

©Copyright 2021 - All rights reserved.

Emotional Self-Care for Black Women

Table of Contents

4 FREE Gifts

To help you along your spiritual journey, I've created 4 FREE bonus eBooks.

You can get instant access by signing up to my email newsletter below.

On top of the 4 free books, you will also receive weekly tips along with free book giveaways, discounts, and so much more.

All of these bonuses are 100% free with no strings attached. You don't need to provide any personal information except your email address.

To get your bonus, go to:

https://dreamlifepress.com/four-free-gifts

Or scan the QR code below

Spirit Guides for Beginners: How to Hear the Universe's Call and Communicate with Your Spirit Guide and Guardian Angels

Guided by Moon herself, inspired by her own experiences and knowledge that has been passed down by hundreds of generations for thousands of years, you'll discover everything you need to know to;

- Understanding what the call of the universe is
- How to hear and comprehend it
- Knowing who and what your spirit guides and guardian angels are
- Learning how to connect, start a conversation, and listen to your guides
- How to manifest your dreams with the help of the cosmic source
- Learning how to start living the life you want to live
- And so much more…

2

Law of Attraction: Manifest Your Desire

Learn how to tap into the infinite power of the universe and manifest everything you want in life.

Includes:

- Law of Attraction: Manifest Your Desire ebook
- Law of Attraction Workbook
- Cheat sheets and checklists so make sure you're on the right path

Hoodoo Book of Spells for Beginners: Easy and effective Rootwork, Conjuring, and Protection Spells for Healing and Prosperity

Harness the power of one of the greatest magics. Hoodoo is a powerful force ideal for holding negativity at bay, promoting positivity in all areas in your life, offering protection to the things you love, and ultimately taking control of your destiny.

Inside, you will discover:

- How to get started with Hoodoo in your day-to-day life
- How to use conjuration spells to manifest the life you want to live
- How casting protection spells can help you withstand the toughest of times
- Break cycles of bad luck and promote good fortune throughout your life
- Hoodoo to encourage prosperity and financial stability
- How to heal using Hoodoo magic, both short-term and long-term traumas and troubles
- Remove curses and banish pain, suffering, and negativity from your life
- And so much more...

4

Book of Shadows

A printable PDF to support you in your spiritual transformation.

Within the pages, you will find:

- Potion and tinctures tracking sheet
- Essential oils log pages
- Herbs log pages
- Magical rituals and spiritual body goals checklist
- Tarot reading spread sheets
- Weekly moon and planetary cycle tracker
- And so much more

Get all the resources for FREE by visiting the link below

https://dreamlifepress.com/four-free-gifts

Introduction

When you think of an emotional black woman, the first thing that probably comes to mind is a woman who is angry, bitter, and raging at the whole world. Either that or our minds draw up the vision of a black woman crying pitifully. We don't see emotions in a positive light and unfortunately, I can't say it's our fault. A few years ago, I shared the same sentiments. Sadly, the messages around me reinforced this imagery I had of what an emotional black woman is supposed to look like. I thought crying was the ultimate expression of a woman's emotions. And so do a lot of people, which is why we strongly try to deter our black brothers from finding emotional expression in their tears. We tell them it is womanly and therefore, "weak."

As we fight for gender equality in today's climate, the freedom to cry freely is gradually being frowned upon as well. We have prospective life partners saying things like, they "don't like their women emotionally weak." And when you translate that in 'regular speak,' they mean they don't want a woman who is tearful or expresses herself in any of the ways I mentioned earlier. The problem is not people having standards for what they want in a potential partner. The problem is the narrow perspective we have when it comes to the colorful range of human emotions and feelings, that we assign emotions to specific genders or dictate how each of us should react to these emotions. And worse still, we made it the general definition of what it means to be an emotional black woman.

This is the reason I felt inspired to write this book. I am hoping that at the end of the book, that picture of who we think an emotional black woman is will change. I do this with the expectation that certain important concepts that we have assigned negative labels to will be seen in a new light and will empower us with the knowledge to help us thrive and grow in our respective endeavors.

At the end of this chapter, I want you to understand what emotional health is and what it means to care for your emotional health. The idea that a strong black woman is someone who has succeeded in shutting down her emotions or someone who does not display emotions in ways that are considered weak should be burned and destroyed forever. That narrative is costing us our peace and happiness. We need to care about our emotions.

What is Emotional Self-Care?

I came across the word self-care in a Hollywood movie. The way it was sold to me was basically taking a bath in a tub surrounded by candles, petals, and all that stuff - which is nice, but far from the whole truth. Self-care is way more than having a nice soak in the tub. It is in your attitude towards yourself. It is in your interactions with other people. It is in the words you silently say to yourself when no one else is listening. When your emotional health is neglected, your inner critic assumes control by default. The voice becomes the loudest and if you do not consciously check your inner critic, the message will be negative, and that negativity will consume you.

A quick internet search tells us that emotional self-care is a conscious effort towards identifying and nurturing your true feelings, your conscious inner state, and your emotional intellect. If I was going to phrase this in a cool way, I would say emotional self-care is the quaint art of giving a f**k. As women, we spend a lot of time and effort trying to get other people to care about our feelings when we fail to do the same for ourselves. We shut ourselves down emotionally and expect some knight in shining armor to come and rescue us. This expectation is ridiculous because we are actually in possession of the key to the chains that hold us down. The only way to help ourselves grow emotionally and to maintain stable emotional health is to start caring about our feelings. And to do that, this process must happen in three phases.

Phase One: Correctly Identify Your Feelings

A lot of us have negative emotional flare-ups, but we tend to focus more on the circumstances that created the flare-ups rather than our reaction to those circumstances. From my understanding, emotions are the symptoms of what is going on inside our heads...mentally. When you get a cold, you manifest symptoms like fever, headache, and so on. To treat it, you don't start chasing the environmental factors that probably led to your cold. Instead, you focus your treatment on what is going on with your body.

Emotional self-care works in the same way because when you have an emotional flare-up (whether negative or positive), you must try to identify what you are feeling and why you are feeling it and then determine the next course of action to ensure that you are in a more positive emotional state. We should aspire to manifest more positive emotional flare-ups than negative ones. That is the end goal (I think it should be).

I am not saying that life is meant to be a bed of roses. That is unrealistic. I am saying that when you build your emotional health through self-care, you reach a point where there is very little in life that will cause you to break to a point where you feel that life is no longer worth it. This point is called emotional resilience, and it is at the core of everything we are going to talk about in this book.

Phase Two: Nurture Your Feelings

I struggled with this phase for the longest time because

of my one-track mind. I assumed that nurturing my feelings was akin to fanning the flames of a burning bush; letting it grow, burn, and eventually consuming you. As I reflect on my thoughts from some years ago, I have to admit that I was kinda crazy. Thankfully, contrary to my crazy world of imagination, it simply means understanding what you are feeling and understanding which actions will pacify you. Let me break that down. I struggled with anger a lot. As a black woman living in a world that is clouded by racism, it is difficult not to be angry. One moment you are enjoying life, and then some person or event comes and squashes that moment like a bug because of their prejudices against your skin color. Worse still, you feel helpless to react.

That sense of helplessness feeds anger and I had a lot of it. When I realized that I had to learn to nurture my feelings, I kept thinking, "Am I supposed to grow this anger?" Thankfully I didn't act on that line of thought. Instead, I sat down and processed my anger. Beyond the helplessness, I needed to understand why I was angry. This helped me realize that my anger was mostly because I felt like my rights were being violated. It was during this process that I also understood that anger is not the negative emotion we have painted it out to be.

It is the way you act when you're angry that brings about negativity.

When I understood that my fundamental rights as a human being were being trampled on and that this is what inspired my anger, I was able to channel that rage into more positive forms that yielded better results (this did not happen overnight). These actions pacified my anger and I learned to embrace my anger because it made me more aware of myself as a woman. Through it, I understood the things I could tolerate in a relationship. It also helped me build clearer boundaries in my relationships. We'll get into this later.

By nurturing your emotions, you develop a better understanding of yourself which will, in turn, help you build better relationships with others.

Phase Three: Conscious Effort

This phase is present from the moment you decide to practice emotional self-care because it requires conscious effort. I am sad to say this, but the reality is that a lot of us are not raised with the knowledge of emotional self-care. We are groomed to survive the physical hardships of this world, but most of us are not lucky enough to have the kind of foundation that helps us prioritize our emotional health. And so, to get into the practice of emotional self-care, we need to make a conscious effort. Another reason conscious effort is important is because of our mental programming. We see the world through our society's lens, which also influences our perception of self. However, nine times out of ten, we are not who society says we are.

It is our duty to take the time to get to know ourselves, understand our visions, and build our goals. All this requires a level of self-awareness and conscious effort to make it happen. As you become more self-aware, you still need to apply more effort to get rid of the preconceived notions you have about how life is supposed to be or how you are supposed to react emotionally in different situations. For example, as black women, we are conditioned to believe that a relationship where love hurts is the one that proves your womanhood. This should never be the case. We deserve men who love us, respect us, and treat us like the queens that we are. However, if you don't make the conscious effort to apply this knowledge in your relationship with yourself as well as the ones you have with other people, you find yourself repeating old negative patterns that bring pain and hurt.

How Does Emotional Self-Care Impact Us?

From my personal experience, I didn't start living - and I mean really living - until I started practicing emotional self-care. Up until that point, I felt as though I was living my life for other people on their terms. I was so afraid to write a book because I was worried about what other people were going to think about me. I stopped myself from taking risks and going on adventures because I allowed the views and opinions of other people to dictate what should or shouldn't be done with my life and my money. But that is just scratching the surface of what you stand to gain when you imbibe the culture of emotional self-care. There are so many benefits but I am only going to focus on 3 of them.

1. Freedom to be you.

We all know those crazy house rules; girls should be this... girls should not do that ...and so on. With emotional self-care, you can break free from those stupid rules and focus on yourself. It is through this that you can understand what your true limitations are and most importantly, unveil your amazing potential. When you invest in your emotional health, you cast yourself in a new light, where you find that those things that were thrust on you or taken away from you because of your gender might hold the key to unlocking the life you dream of.

Sometimes, the freedom you gain is simply finding validation in your emotional expressions. You may discover that you are not the crazy girlfriend they said you were. You were simply expressing your emotional need, which is crucial to your existence in any relationship.

2. Emotional Intelligence

Emotional intelligence goes beyond your ability to recognize other people's emotions. How you act on the knowledge that you have defines the level of your emotional intelligence. Through emotional self-care, you are able to develop a deeper understanding of emotions, and this gives you a greater ability to connect with people who might be going through similar circumstances. And it is through these connections that you are able to develop deeper bonds with people, giving you the chance to build more sustainable relationships.

3. Self-awareness

Without proper emotional self-care, it is almost impossible to determine how well you know yourself. If you simply accept the labels that people throw on you based on their limited understanding of who you are, you are depriving yourself of the opportunity to explore the depths of your personality and everything that comes with being you. One major contributor to poor self-esteem is an absence of self-awareness. When you don't know who you are, you accept whatever is given to you, and often, you get the crumbs that fall off the table. This negatively impacts your self-esteem.

Why is Emotional Self-Care Crucial for a Better Life as a Black Woman?

The crusade for better emotional self-care for black women should have started hundreds of years ago. Right now, as the world veers into chaos thanks to the raging pandemic and other disturbing social factors, it is even more important for us black women to band up together and look inwards for the solutions that the world needs today. The starting point for any tangible solution in any given society is self-reflection. Being a black woman in today's world means a lot of things to different people, but factually speaking, our role in society is crucial. We hold up families and empires, and their continued existence is dependent on us getting it right with ourselves.

We have put everyone else ahead of ourselves and this has been to our detriment. We have become more broken than ever, and broken people only end up breaking other people. Through emotional self-care, we can start putting those pieces back together and mending those areas of our lives that require it. We need deep healing in our community, and as women of color, that inner hurt has a lot to do with the negative messages we have been raised with or around. Through conscious efforts on our part, we can become more self-aware. This will help us grow into our power and potential and through this power, we can begin initiating the transformation we want to see in the world around us today. It is time to come out of denial. It is time to shed the lies. But most importantly, it is time to take up our rightful places in society. And the fact is, we can only do that from an emotionally healthy place. Having this in mind, let's explore emotional health in detail.

CHAPTER ONE

The Core Layers of Emotional Health

The entire purpose of this book is to bring your complete focus to yourself. No other chapter in this book will demand this of you more than this first chapter. Here, we are looking inwards, and you need to brace yourself for information you might be subconsciously aware of but are not emotionally ready for. We tend to avoid these topics because we don't like how they make us feel. But we must understand that emotional self-care is about acknowledging your feelings and tending to them. These feelings are not always going to be pleasant but it's okay. Life is not all sunshine and rainbows. We have days where the clouds are dark and scary, but those days bring us the rain that turns the land lush and green.

With a better understanding of self, you can turn those dark and unpleasant emotions into pointers that direct you on a path that is more ideal for you and the life you want. When I started my emotional self-care journey, one of the things that helped me was having a vision of what my end goal was. I wanted a life where I was happier because I was doing the things that I loved and experiencing those things with people who love me just as much as I loved them. I found that paying attention to the causes of those negative emotions I was experiencing helped me to identify the things I really wanted in my life and the things that I had outgrown. And I believe that this was how I was able to get to the point where my life is everything that I wanted to be.

Side note; I need you to constantly remind yourself that having the life that you want doesn't mean having a perfect life. The objective is having a life that is so amazing that even on dark days, it fits right into the pattern of things. By acknowledging what is important to you, you allow yourself to develop positive solutions to the things that might be causing you emotional problems. When we deny ourselves what we want without developing self-awareness, the problem doesn't fade away or disappear. It simply builds up to a point where it becomes toxic. It is like covering a can of spoiled milk. Just because it's covered up and tucked away in a corner doesn't mean that the milk stops being bad. It just gets worse. The same thing happens to our emotions when we don't tend to them properly.

In this chapter, we are going to look at the three core aspects of emotional health. We will start with self-awareness, which is knowledge of who you are. We will then explore self-esteem, which emphasizes how you feel about who you are. And finally, we have self-efficiency, which is basically how you service your feelings about yourself based on the knowledge you have about your identity to improve your life and make it better. Is this making you scratch your head a little bit? Hang in there. Everything will become clearer in a bit as we address these core areas one by one.

Self-Awareness

When you put aside your title at work, your relationship status, and whatever wealth you may or may not have accumulated throughout your entire existence, ask yourself, who are you? Many of us, for a lot of wrong reasons, have attached our identity to the things that we own, the people we associate with, and the work we do. These are all important in their own way. The relationships you have provide you with the unit you need to thrive. The work you do gives expression to your skills and talents. The things you own are basically your way of expressing delight and joy. However, no matter how grand, amazing, or terrible all these things are, they cannot give depth or definition to your identity. That is something that comes from within.

We live in a world that is obsessed with labels, but we shy away from the most important label all of us carry - the label of self. These other labels that we choose to carry come with expectations. There is the single mum label, the patient wife label, and the independent woman label, just to mention a few. While these labels may fit us perfectly, we tend to attach more meaning to the social expectations that come with these labels. For example, there is a societal expectation of what a successful woman should look like. As a result, many of us are unable to identify as successful because we feel that we don't fit into that image of success. This is where self-awareness comes into play. It is imperative that you know what your goals are in life.

I am not talking about goals that you inherited from your parents or people that you looked up to. I am talking about goals that give you a sense of purpose and a sense of accomplishment. These are goals that tend to your innermost needs and desires. They come from a place of selfish expectations. The word 'selfish' used to make me cringe before, and that was because I only associated it with negative emotions. However, when you start your self-reflective journey and look inwards, you cannot honestly do a good job of it without being a little selfish. This means disregarding the messages you have been groomed with right from when you were a child and focusing solely on your needs and wants. It is from this place that we can now define what our goals are. It is from here you can truly paint a picture of what you want your future to look like, and it is here that you will begin to see the blessings you already have.

So, take the time to get to know yourself. Don't rush the process. Don't sweep anything under the rug. Ask those pertinent questions. Be honest in your answers and layer by layer, you will reveal the person hiding behind the unnecessary labels.

Self-Esteem

Knowing who you are is one aspect of your journey. How you feel about this person you now know is a completely different story. Your self-esteem is basically your feelings towards your perception of self. If you don't feel good about who you are, you are bound to experience poor self-esteem. Poor self-esteem is not a direct result of the absence of certain things in your life. It is the dissatisfaction or our inability to truly accept the real and honest version of ourselves. It is possible to accept who you are and then decide to make changes so that you can grow into the person you want to become. However, if you focus solely on becoming a totally different person without trying to be more self-aware and understanding who you are, you may end up constantly making changes and never being satisfied.

Up until a few years ago, the beauty of being black was not deeply appreciated. In the media, people with light skin color were being appreciated over their counterparts. I remember being completely unaware that a particular country had people with darker skin shade until I visited. My misinformation was largely due to what was portrayed in the media. It wasn't surprising to find that brown boys and girls in that country felt the need to undergo cosmetic procedures to lighten their skin. As black women, we are constantly made to feel like we are not good enough no matter how hard we try. The struggle to succeed has become so 'normal' that we think it is okay for black women to work twice as hard as their colleagues just to get less than half of what they deserve.

The acceptance of unfair practices as the norm shouldn't minimize our self-discovery journey, but it does a terrible number on our self-esteem. We are made to feel like we should be competing against our peers when our only competition should be ourselves. Imagine running a race where everything is about the person running beside you. The crowd is waving their flags and chanting their names. Even the people officiating the race seem to be rooting for everyone but you. It gets to a point where you feel that the race is about them and you are invisible. That is what happens when you are not self-aware. You become invisible to the point where your self-esteem is non-existent. You need to stop and embrace every feeling you have about yourself...Good, bad...everything. This will help you embrace the idea of loving yourself at your worst and at your best. That is where the idea of unconditional love stems from. You don't need to be someone or something to appreciate your unique qualities. It is through the acceptance of every aspect of yourself that you can start building a healthy self-esteem.

Self-Efficiency

When you know who you are and how you feel about who you are, the next logical step on that journey is taking actions to get where you want to be. This is what self-efficiency is about. I used to think that self-efficiency was about performing some form of service for other people. Or being resourceful enough. However, in this context, it is much more than that. By understanding the knowledge you have gained about yourself and the feelings you have about that knowledge, you can take the necessary action to create the future you desire. Let's say you have become aware of your unhealthy eating habits and when you look at yourself in the mirror, you see the outcome of those eating habits. But instead of hating yourself for it, you come up with an actionable plan that will help you work towards the body you desire. This is what self-efficiency is about.

On your journey to becoming emotionally healthier, you need to learn to cater to your emotions. Catering to your emotions does not mean indulging in every feeling you have. Self-efficiency helps you cater to your emotions using knowledge as opposed to instinct. We do some things instinctively, but self-efficiency is about putting considerable thought into the actions we intend to take before we take them.

Practicing self-efficiency in emotional self-care can be as simple as letting go. Using the example of unhealthy eating habits, letting go of the repressed emotions you are trying to drown out with food is a self-efficient/sufficient act. It allows you to use your knowledge of the cause of the bad habit, and make changes by letting go. It also serves your self-esteem because you are no longer powerless to the urge to eat whenever you have an emotional crisis. Instead, you are putting yourself in a position of power by taking the right steps to become a much better version of yourself.

For me, self-efficiency is about staying true to my happiness, connecting myself to actions, thoughts, and words that empower me and make me feel visible in my world. Being self-sufficient is allowing yourself to be confident in your choices and goals. To be truly self-sufficient, you must let go of any past trauma that has defined you - it could be a mistake that you made or something that was done to you as a child or even as an adult. Holding on to pain makes it difficult for you to uproot the things in your life that have kept you caged in, and they will keep empowering your inner critic. Your inner critic convinces you that you can't do this or you shouldn't do that because of "imagined" reasons or experiences. Holding onto emotions like guilt only give your inner critic more material to use against you.

As we wrap up this chapter and move on, here is a task for you:

1. Do the work. Don't procrastinate. Don't try to rush it. Just do the work.

2. Embrace yourself. Literally. Hug yourself and be grateful for being you.

3. Let it go. The hurt, the disappointment, all of it. Let it go.

When you complete these tasks, you will find yourself at the end. The best part of the process is falling in love with who you are and the person you are becoming.

CHAPTER TWO

Building Your Perception of Self

After undergoing intensive self-evaluation, you may find yourself wanting in some areas. Just because you are meant to embrace every facet of who you are does not mean that you are perfect and without flaws. This acceptance is a critical part of the process of loving yourself unconditionally as self-love is not and should not be attached to certain expectations of one's self. However, self-improvement is an important part of the self-love journey. The love you express towards yourself doesn't involve just being kinder to yourself, but also wanting better for yourself.

This brings us to the subject of this chapter - building your perception of self.

Your perception of self will define your self-esteem. One of my favorite Instagram accounts features a duck that acts like a dog because it was raised among 5 dogs. When the duck is with his 5 brothers, the only people who think it's a duck are you and I. While the self-delusion of this sweet duck is not exactly a fine example, it highlights how your perception of self can inflate your confidence and help you stand strong against other people's opinions. When it comes to your identity, you are the only person with the right to control the narrative. People are entitled to their own opinions, but the person whose opinions ultimately define you is you.

In this chapter, we are going to learn how to separate your identity from other people's perceptions of who you are. You will shed those layers of your identity that are built on lies and other false representations. Raising your self-esteem is important. When you look into the mirror every day, does your reflection represent everything you are or everything you despise? The way you feel indicates how high or low your self-perception meter is.

By the end of this chapter, I want you to be able to think highly of yourself. Stop coming up with excuses to be anything less than the best. You deserve so much better, but you can't expect other people to do what you have failed to do for yourself. If you are ready to give your image a boost, let's start with the most obvious part: uncovering the lies.

Uncover the Lies

As black women, our identity is masked under layers of images projected onto us by other people. You start as daddy's girl. Then you become Paul's woman. If things go according to plan, you become Rebecca's mother. These kinds of tags are also found in official places. Your name is not enough for people. They put you in a box because it helps them feel like they've figured you out.

Instead of investing the time and effort it takes to know someone and then figuring them out, people prefer to identify you using official titles such as Ronson's PA or the company's accountant. These are not essentially wrong when you look at them from a very simple context. However, by placing these labels on you, there is also an expectation of how they think you should think and behave.

These expectations become the lies we use to clothe ourselves and they form an integral part of our identity. We no longer look at our situations logically because we believe there is a standard that has been set and we are supposed to live up to them based on the identity given to us. To be a daddy's girl, you are expected to depend on your father for virtually everything because the idea of an independent woman being a daddy's girl is unheard of. In the same way, the personal assistant of a prominent male figure is expected to bend to her boss's will even when they cross her personal space and, in some cases, abuse the employee/employer relationship. When you find yourself at a crossroad where your morals or value system do not align with the expectation of the identity you have been given, you start questioning yourself rather than the social ideals that put you in that box.

Questioning the social ideals that have put you in a mental quagmire helps you uncover what is real about you and what isn't. This is where you start questioning the reason people expect you to behave and speak a certain way because you are a black woman. You can be a daddy's girl and still be strong, fierce, and independent.

It is possible to be a daddy's girl and not bow down to the patriarchy that expects you to be a helpless damsel-in-distress. Whatever position you occupy in society, the burden of responsibility falls on you to define how you interpret that role. Yes, there are standard expectations pertaining to the duties we are expected to perform. However, those roles should not form your identity. Understand your limitations physically and mentally, and then use that to determine how it plays into your identity. Don't let people push their own version of your identity on you.

Embrace the Truth

Have you ever entered an empty home and felt the presence of the people who were there before? My grandfather used to tell me that if you clear out a house and don't fill it up afterward, it will echo what was there before you took it out. In other words, if your sole purpose was to get rid of certain items in the house and you don't replace those items with the things you want, there will be an echo of what was there before. The only way to counteract it is to replace it with something else. In the same way, if you get rid of lies about yourself and you fail to fill up the empty spots with the truth, you will find yourself echoing the lies that were there before. Understand this; when you are in this mental warfare involving what society thinks of you vs what you think of yourself, truth and lies are the most utilized weapons. In the previous segment, our focus was uncovering lies, especially those involving social expectations based on the boxes placed over us by people in our immediate environment.

In this segment, you are encouraged to not only uncover what the truth is, but to embrace it. There is a general cliché; the truth hurts. This is only true to some extent. The truth is only harmful when its sole intention is to hurt the recipient of that truth. Now, this is a self-assessment task, and the objective is to empower yourself. Therefore, the truth you uncover during this process will not hurt you, but empower you. The process of increasing your self-power requires a little bit of unpleasantness, but not the kind that brings about pain. It simply takes you away from your comfort zone. When you confront yourself with certain truths about your identity, you may have to think uncomfortable thoughts. The only reason those thoughts are uncomfortable is because you were raised in a specific way, and the truth might force you to go against what you believe are your ideologies in life.

The truth forces you to broaden your perspectives. It gives you more than one view at a time and it is from these different perspectives that you get more information about the person you are. It's like having a high-performance computer in the hands of a person who is clueless about computers. They will use it for basic tasks, and the computer will never be utilized to its full potential. But in the hands of a tech whiz, that computer becomes a massive instrument for doing amazing things. That's what knowing the truth about yourself does. This in turn will help you build up your perception of self.

As strange as the truth may seem and as uncomfortable as it may feel, you need to put yourself in a frame of mind to accept this new truth. For example, women have been called the weaker vessel for years simply because society says so. However, when you look at your journey through life and the things that you have accomplished up to this point, you will find that there is power in being a woman. This truth may not feel comfortable to other people. It may not even feel comfortable for you, but if you are going to learn the new truth, you must embrace it.

Rebrand your Identity

Whenever I think of rebranding and identity, the first image that comes to mind is that of the Coca-Cola bottle. This is a brand that has been around for over a century, and they consistently put themselves out there. It is almost hard to believe that this was a drink invented by a doctor, exclusively sold in a pharmacy and that at one time it was believed to cure coughs. As the times evolved and policies changed, the company rebranded and made itself to be a drink that contained happiness. Whether this is true or not is not up for debate. This was a story they sold us, and the entire world bought into it because Coca-Cola is now a global brand. That is the power of rebranding your identity: you tell people your story, not the other way around.

So far, you have uncovered lies about who you are and exposed some truths about yourself. The next step in this journey is to merge the truth with your expectations for yourself. Word of caution - this is not where you go overboard with your ideas. What do I mean by going overboard? You may want to lose some weight. That is something to aspire to, but deciding to lose 50 pounds in 3 days is going overboard. You are free to dream. There is no need to put a limit on what you can be. Just make sure that the new identity does not end up breaking you in the process. If you are going to set a body goal or beauty goal, make sure that you are doing it for yourself. This is very important because we've just left a place where our identity was shaped by the opinion and perspectives of other people. Now that you have a chance to rebrand, don't repeat the same mistakes.

So, how do you rebrand? First of all, sit down. Take a minute and think about the woman you want to become. Picture how she lives her life every day from the moment she wakes up. Think about what time this woman wakes up, the kind of activities she indulges in from sunrise to sundown. Think about how she dresses and while you are picturing these things, imagine how you'd feel while doing those things. This is important because you are entering into a new age within yourself where your happiness is the priority. If you are going to live your life on your terms, your rebranding should be about becoming a person who makes you feel even better about yourself. The key to achieving this is to ensure that this new image is built on the truth about yourself and the things that trigger positive emotions. It should never be about what people think you should look or live like.

CHAPTER THREE

Attain Emotional Balance

Emotional balance in my opinion refers to the ability to effectively manage your emotions in an honest and healthy way. People think that not reacting to your emotions makes you emotionally balanced. Or the fact that you don't feel negative emotions speaks to your emotional maturity. This is all wrong. We are human. One of our defining markers as human beings is emotions. We are made to feel and experience life as it happens to us. And sometimes, we need to react to these emotions to fully explore the experiences around us. Failure to do so creates an imbalance in your emotional life and where there is an emotional imbalance, it is difficult for you to step into your identity as a powerful black woman who has healed from the trauma and is ascending into her awesomeness.

When I defined emotional balance, I used two words that the hallmark of true emotional balance; 'honesty' and 'healthy.' You need to be honest about what you are feeling and then ensure that you are reacting to those feelings in a healthy way. But before you can be honest about what you are feeling, you must be aware. And that is a theme that you will find throughout this book. You cannot afford to live your life in a default setting where you act and react on instinct. It is even worse when you realize that the instincts we are acting on were written in our DNA millions of years ago. This was at a time when life was completely different from the way it is now and the secondary foundation for our instinct is the environment that we find ourselves in. So, when you rely on instinct you are relying on outdated survival strategies biologically embedded in us. This means that you may not be acting on what is best for you.

In this chapter, I am going to explore what it means to be fully aware of what we feel. This includes asking the necessary questions of 'what.' Questions like, what am I feeling? Why do I feel this way? Through the answers that we get, we may be able to uncover the underlying fears that have held us bound and empowered the inner critic within us. When we are aware, we become honest about our feelings. It is crazy that we have made it okay to deny what we feel based on some social expectation placed on gender. For example, men are not supposed to cry and women are too emotional. So, because we want to avoid these labels, we deny our feelings. But no more. To attain emotional balance, you must be honest with what you are feeling and learn to react to those emotions healthily.

Confront your Fears

One of the craziest things I learned on my journey was the fact that fear is not a negative emotion per se. It is how we react to it that creates a negative experience. There is no true emotion that is negative. It is our reaction to them that causes the negativity. If you react to positive emotions like love and happiness negatively, you will get a negative outcome. And yes, it is possible to react to love negatively. However, this is not the subject of this chapter. Our focus is on this thing called fear. Oftentimes, when we are planted in an environment that takes us out of our comfort zone, the first emotion that emerges is fear and this fear has a way of pushing us to exercise caution before making a decision. Ultimately, it is about protecting your interests. When you understand that fear comes from a place of self-preservation, you start building a different attitude towards it.

You should realize that by protecting yourself, you are limiting yourself from fulfilling your potential, which means that fear has taken control. In such a scenario, fear is no longer serving you. It has become a hindrance. To counteract this, it is important to explore the fears that you have entertained in your life. Sometimes fear is a result of direct or indirect experiences. When you exercise caution in your dealings, pause to ask critical questions such as 'the whys.' Why are you doing this? Why are you not doing that? When you understand the reason behind your action, fear no longer becomes a barrier but rather an ally on your journey. You get to understand just how far you need to exercise caution. Is it going to take you to the first three steps or the next 50 steps? If you find that your fears are based on irrational things or outdated theories, then it is time to reevaluate your choices so that you can take the bold steps that you need to get to the next level.

People like to use grand terms such as slaying your dragons to define confronting your fears. It makes it seem as though you are doing something monumental, and this can hinder you from taking a step. The best way to approach this is to question yourself. Asking the right questions forces us to change perspectives and leads us to a credible reason. And until you can accurately identify a reason that resonates with your being, you must keep pushing forward. The scariest step is the first step you take. When you take that first step and realize that the fears are not what you made them out to be, it becomes easier to take the next step and the next one until you get to a conclusive end. Another fear you need to conquer is the fear of failure. A lot of black women hold themselves back because they are afraid of what will happen if they fail. You need to understand that failure is not a defining experience. It provides you with lessons if you look beyond the pain or negative emotions evoked by that failure. My mentor always told me that the fear of failure is the cage for potential. If you really want to be the woman you think you are meant to be, you must let go of this fear.

Take Down Those Emotional Walls

As women, when we experience a negative emotion because of heartbreak, betrayal, or disappointment, we resolve to shut down emotionally because we feel if we have our emotional walls up, nobody can hurt us. In theory, this sounds good. Take away the emotions and you take away the pain that these emotions cause. But the trade-off is that it deprives us of the privilege and joys of truly living life. Without emotions, we become empty entities who are just existing; unable to connect on a deeper level with the people around us. Yes, betrayal is painful. When you love someone and trust them and then they turn around and stab you in the back, that pain hurts like nothing else. But guess what? That is part of our experiences as humans.

Is it possible to live a life without heartbreak? Probably. But you would have to be the most cautious person in the world or the luckiest. However, if you spend your life protecting yourself from heartbreaks, you end up protecting yourself from other important emotions like genuine kindness, love, or happiness. You would find it difficult to let people into your life. It is the people that you let into your life who will give you rich memories to last you a lifetime. If you are going to silence your inner critic, you need to learn to take down those walls. it is scary to put yourself out there in a world that seems vile and full of hate. But you need to understand that there is also love out there. There are also people who will fill your life with so much enjoyment that you will thank the pain you experienced in the past because it led you to this point.

The truth is you deserve to live a life of joy. You deserve to love and be loved. You deserve to be in relationships with people who honor you and respect you. But those kinds of situations can only happen when you let yourself be loved. When you put up an emotional wall, you shut out the rest of the world. You may successfully shut out those negative emotions you are trying to avoid but you will certainly also shut out happiness. I am not saying that you cannot find happiness within. But if you are going to accept the truth, you must accept all of it. And one important truth is that we rely on our fellow humans for a full and healthy life experience. Just remember that letting down those emotional walls does not mean you have to be stupid about the choices you make. We will get to that in a subsequent chapter where you learn about setting healthy boundaries in any relationship. But for now, accept that opening yourself up is the only way you are going to be able to receive what you are expecting.

Be Vulnerable

One of my favorite movies to watch with my girls is

friends with benefits. It is a movie that showcases the need for vulnerability in our relationships. These two people came together because they felt an immense attraction to each other. However, because of their past relationships and the negative experiences they had, they decided they wanted a relationship where emotions were strictly regulated. They were just going to be two people smashing whenever they felt the urge but without the emotional complications that come with relationships. The problem with this arrangement from the onset was the fact that they were friends first. When you are friends with someone, there is an emotional connection. It is a wasted effort to attempt to enter a 'situationship' with a friend.

It is like saying you are going to buy your favorite cake in the world, store it in the fridge and not eat it. Especially when you refuse to stock your fridge up with any alternative food. It is a disaster waiting to happen. Being vulnerable in today's world is often interpreted as being weak. People think that being vulnerable sets you up for disappointment. Yet when they get into relationships, they expect people to be able to read their minds, know what they want, and offer it to them. This is impossible. Being vulnerable is about expressing your expectations to others. It is as simple as that. Now, being vulnerable doesn't mean loving someone to stupidity. That is just dumb behavior. Let's say, for example, you sign up on a dating app. On such platforms, you will find all kinds of people; people who just want to have sex, people who want to have conversations, and even people with more sinister objectives.

Being vulnerable on such a platform is not putting up your house address and your monthly income details so that people know you for what you have. That is crazy. The right way to be vulnerable is to let people know what you expect out of whatever relationships you form. Sure, some people may want to prey on this information you have provided so that they can get what they want from you. We will talk about this in another chapter. But for now, remember what we said about the fear of failure and how that cages your potential. When you decide to withhold information that is critical to the success of any relationship you build because you are afraid that someone is going to take advantage of it, you are killing the potential to find a prospective date. This applies to other areas of your life. Being vulnerable is essentially putting your intentions out there and having the courage to stick to your principles by only settling for what you want. Nothing more and nothing less.

Being vulnerable is a different kind of strength and as we go into the next chapter to discuss the darkness within, you will understand just how powerful being vulnerable is.

Chapter Four

The Battle Within

To become an empowered black woman who not only survives the world we live in today but thrives amid the chaos, you must look inward for strength. However, because of our messed-up backgrounds, crazy experiences, and even crazier self-imposed expectations, there is a war raging within that must be won if we are going to give ourselves a chance in this life. This war is borne out of an emotional conflict that arises when our sense of self clashes with the projection of other people's expectations of us.

In this chapter, we are going to look at three major sources of this battle: anxiety, depression, and anger.

Almost every black woman that I know has had their life's experiences clouded by one or all these emotions.

We are made to feel like there are specific things we must have and without them, we cannot be considered wholesome. For example, a woman in her thirties, unmarried, and without children is often regarded as incomplete, and this lack of completeness makes us feel like failures. By our own standards, we can call ourselves successful and accomplished women. But in the presence of other people, our accomplishments diminish because there is an expectation of who we should be, and this leaves us worried. As if our black girl struggles aren't enough today, our pain is often silenced. There are cases of black women who go missing for months and years before law enforcement agencies take the reports seriously. This lackadaisical attitude towards our welfare and absence of safety damages us physically and emotionally. And worse, because we are often put in this situation by the very people who are supposed to have our best interest at heart, this creates another form of anxiety.

However, I want you to know that because this is a common experience doesn't mean that it has to define your personal experience as a black woman. Yes, there are social prejudices, injustices, and other things that we will talk about in this book. But for now, you should put the focus on yourself, your journey, your experience, and how you can tackle what is going on within. This way, you can get to the light that is inside you and through that light, illuminate your essence and share that light with the rest of the world. That is the objective of this book. At the end of the day, I want to see you shine. I want to see you rise above your fears, your failures, and whatever limitation society has placed on you. I want you to be able to open your mouth and tell the world, "I am a successful black woman," and mean it with every fiber of your being. To do that, we must tackle these three emotions that have eaten into the heart of our community as black women.

Anxiety

Anxiety has become a buzzword in our world. It is so common for people to use the word that you would be forgiven for assuming that it is a trend. However, as "trendy" as it may sound, anxiety is something that has been around for eons. The major difference between past and present anxiety is that it is documented a lot more now. Also, people own up to their anxiety. But what exactly is this anxiety? And how/why is its impact on the black community, particularly its women, so vital to your transformation journey? Before we get into it, let me remind you that I am no expert on the subject. I am coming at it from my experience as well as those of people close to me. The clinical data on anxiety can be found on the internet, in books, and so on. Anxiety in lay terms from the perspective of someone who lived with it for years and learned to manage is what you are going to get here. So, with that in mind, let us get into it.

In my opinion, anxiety is the body's exaggerated response to worry and concern. However, it is not as simple as it sounds. Nothing ever is. When you are anxious, your biological fight or flight response is activated. Your emotions are so alert that they initiate a physical response. That worry and concern are expressed as elevated heart rate, short breaths, and other accompanying physical symptoms. It is interesting to note that this fear is not always based on reality. It is often either your mind reliving an experience or anticipating a negative outcome. I am not great at social interactions. I love being around people, but the thought of talking to people verbally or nonverbally makes me anxious. The root cause of my anxiety was tumbling down on stage when I was 7. Every time I get thrown into a social situation, I fear that I am going to end up falling flat on my face. In essence, my anxiety is not based on real-time events. Generally, anxiety latches on to fear, amplifies it, and then cripples you from the inside.

In our community, we believe in actual events. When you are anxious because there is the presence of real danger or cause for concern in your environment, you get sympathy from people. But reacting to the concern without any physical evidence to support the cause for your worries will attract criticisms and harsh judgments that will further trigger your anxiety. Many black women have to appear strong. We are encouraged to suppress our fears when the only outcome is the massive growth of those fears leading to years of emotional torture. The objective shouldn't be to ignore your fears, but refusing to let them control your actions. We must teach ourselves to explore our fears. Uncover their source and the rationale behind them. Listen to your body. Don't judge yourself based on what you think other people are going to think or say. Most importantly, don't doubt yourself. Your fears and concerns are real. But they should not take control of your life.

Depression

Life is full of ups and downs. This is a slogan that you have probably come across. Depression kind of works the same way, except there are more lows than highs. Being sad occasionally is perfectly normal. It is a natural response to the pain of loss. And loss is something we all deal with at some point in our lives. The gravity of loss we experience will determine how much grieving we go through. But our ability to effectively manage our sadness. Without this ability, when we hit those low points in life, our reaction to it would drag us even lower. Depression is like a constant dark cloud on what should be a bright and sunny day. Some people have described it as a constant weight on their shoulders. Like drowning with weights attached to the feet. It is a horrible description but the sense of helplessness that comes with it makes it even worse.

Our community is riddled with losses. Preventable but painful losses nonetheless. The racial injustice and prejudices which make day-to-day living tedious has become "acceptable." In fact, some people go as far as justifying such treatment being meted out to people they consider different. When you take into consideration the challenges that come with life generally and being a black woman, the odds are stacked against you. This creates a perfect environment for overwhelming sadness that may transform into depression. Because virtually everyone is experiencing the pain of loss, we are unable to console each other, much less ourselves. As a result, we slowly become masters in the art of mourning. We learn to cope with the pain but rarely learn to heal. Sadly, we pass on this lifestyle of mourning to the next generation, and the cycle continues. This doesn't have to be your story.

Overcoming depression is not about getting over your pain. It lies in true healing. The cliche, "time heals all wounds" cannot be true if you do not use the time to initiate the steps to healing. Burying your pain can provide reprieve but it does not give you the necessary skills to efficiently manage pain, loss, and grief. If you are going to get past that negative inner voice, you must learn to manage your reaction to the downs and low points in life. Grief or loss management is an essential life skill to reach our full potential. I wish that life was all roses and no thorns. But if you only mentally prepare yourself for the good parts in life, you leave yourself exceptionally vulnerable when those not-so-great parts come along.

Anger

Anger is an emotion that has gotten a negative rap. People feel that anger is something that shouldn't be experienced at all when in reality, it is crucial for a healthy life experience. Anger is a biological way of letting you know that someone has violated your rights. It doesn't always mean that you are right. It just means that you have certain subconscious lines and someone may have crossed them, making you angry. Anger is not bad. As I said, I don't believe in negative emotions. However, our reaction to these emotions is what we qualify as negative or positive. When you flare up in anger and aggressively attack other people, your anger becomes negative. But when you learn to manage anger effectively and react to it appropriately, your anger becomes a powerful ally.

Our current perspective regarding anger is fueled by what we have witnessed in our community. We see anger in its raw and excessive form. This makes it difficult for us to understand this complex emotion and learn how to manage it. We are not supposed to silence our anger or pretend it's not real. At the same time, we are not supposed to give in to the rage that we feel every time it comes over us. In our community, we frown upon the concept of anger management because we believe it connotes weakness. Ironically, it is the excessive display of rage that is often applauded, especially in men. In women, it is entertained. They call us spicy for being expressive with our anger until we slight them. Then they call us bitches. Neither of these attitudes is healthy. We need a more beneficial approach to addressing our anger.

As a black woman, I understand your anger. We have been unjustly treated by society. The men that are supposed to love and protect us end up abusing us and this has created a lot of anger. Not to mention the anger that we inherited from the pains our ancestors experienced. We have a lot of healing to do as a community. But before we get to that point, we need to start by healing individually. The healing process begins with understanding how to manage your feelings, especially anger. It is okay to be angry but don't let it get to the point of rage. In the process of managing your anger, you should try not to put the expectations of other people before your feelings. Yes, anger should be controlled. But don't forget that anger lets you know when your personal space or lines have been violated.

It is important to react (in a healthy way of course) so that you can set those boundaries and maintain a space that is conducive for your mental and physical health. Don't entertain the antics of other people simply because you want to manage your anger. Be rational in your reaction but ensure that you do acknowledge that emotion, its cause, and perhaps the solution. And speaking of causes, one of the underlying root sources of the anger that is embedded deep into our community today is the racial wall that has forced us to live like outcasts within our own community. People look at us and resort to their prejudices and biases before getting to know us. This has led to unfair treatment and a lot of injustice. I don't have to outline the struggles we have had to face in various societies simply because of the color of our skin. The next chapter educates us on how to manage social expectations based on skin color and gender. It doesn't excuse the behavior or attitude society has towards us. It simply educates us on how to function and thrive under those ugly circumstances.

CHAPTER FIVE

The Race War

Humans are communal by nature. We are biologically programmed to share our spaces with each other. However, some conditions must be met for this to happen. One of those conditions is sharing similarities. We erroneously believe that to tolerate and live peacefully with each other, we must look, think, and act alike. Anyone different from us is an outsider and therefore not deserving of the benefits of being a part of a community. As disheartening as this sounds, this is not even the worst part. For some reason, we have decided that certain qualities merit a person having or being worth more than others. These qualities are embedded in the color of our skin, the size of our wallets, and even in the language we speak.

The idea that one race is inherently superior to another has led to world wars. And even though we have extinguished the flames of the last three wars, the battle continues. There are people who feel that they are entitled to specific benefits simply because their skin has a lighter hue. They strongly believe that people with darker skin color are inferior and next to animals. Therefore, they shouldn't be a part of society. This led to the birth of a system that actively antagonizes people of color. This is ironic because we live in a society that is diverse and evidently, one that has benefited immensely from our diversity. Yet, some people feel that those benefits should be allocated to white people.

There have been several attempts to raise awareness about this injustice. Our ancestors as well as people who have noticed the absurdity of this race war have protested for hundreds of years. But still, it prevails in society. The statistics that highlight the impact of the racial war against people of color are mind-boggling and baffling. Our community has suffered losses, pains, heartaches, and severe mental breakdowns. Despite speaking out against people who choose to oppress us, not much has changed. Granted, things aren't the same as they used to be, but change has been terribly slow. However, some people have managed to thrive under such conditions without losing their sense of self and integrity. In this chapter, we are going to learn how to do the same.

Damaging Social Misconceptions

Our first opinion of self is developed during the first few years of our existence. The people we interact with and the community we live in plays a huge role in defining our perception of self. I talked about this earlier and now you'll see how this plays out. There are a lot of damaging social misconceptions about being a black woman. And because these things are repeated in the content we consume, it is not surprising that many of us absorb these messages and use them as our identity. I am going to talk about three of some of the most damaging social misconceptions about women of color.

1. Tolerating Abuse is a Mark of Strength

Black women are inherently strong. This is one of our superpowers. We are physically, emotionally, and mentally strong. However, the definition of that strength has been miscommunicated to us. When we are put in relationships, one of the things that is expected of us is long-suffering with emphasis on the last part. A woman of virtue is described as a woman who endures all the excesses of her husband in the hopes of having his love as a reward for her endurance.

Loyalty is preached in relationships but in our community, it is a lopsided expectation in the sense that women are expected to be loyal to their men. But the same loyalty is not required from the men. A lot of black women are put in relationships where their partners abuse them physically, mentally, and emotionally and the moment she says she's had enough she is bullied for her decision because society feels she is not displaying strength. This kind of collective thinking has left a lot of women trapped in marriages and relationships that degrade them and make them question their instincts, their emotions, and their sanity. This abuse empowers that negative inner voice we are trying to get rid of. True strength lies in one's ability to relentlessly pursue their goals regardless of the obstacles in their way. It is your ability to rise above your circumstances, not in your ability to endure the cruelty of others.

2. Black Women Are Inferior Species

I am happy that black women are beginning to rediscover the magic we carry within. However, the scars left behind by centuries of racial abuse have embedded the concept of black women being inferior in the minds of a lot of people, including members of our community. Our beauty, our culture, our features, and everything about us is ridiculed because of the color of our skin. With years of reinforcing the same message, it is not surprising that many of us have accepted the idea that we are inferior to women with different skin colors.

We feel that to be accepted, we need to change the way we look and modify our features so that we can blend in with the rest of the world. This is wrong. You are beautiful. You are powerful. Your beauty is the stuff poets write about. If you go to the Bible and read the Songs of Solomon, he was talking about a beautiful black woman. Do you see the lyrics used in that piece? It describes beauty like no other. You need to start seeing yourself in a different light. Woman, you are beautiful.

3. Black Women Are Bound to Fail.

My favorite quote of all time is, "Whether you can or you can't, you are right." Because of the way society has been set up, social structures support people with skin tones different from ours. Meaning that from the moment they are born, they are given the right resources to help them get to their destination effortlessly. People of color, on the other hand, are deprived of basic necessities, making our journey twice as hard and more likely to fail. However, you need to understand that the absence of those resources does not automatically determine the outcome of your life. You are the biggest factor that determines how far you go in life. Yes, it would be easier if you had those resources at your disposal. And yes, we need to work twice as hard just to get by. But that is where our inherent strength comes to play.

While we are working together towards building a society that provides equal opportunity for every one of us, we must forge our own path under the tough circumstances laid out before us. Our strength must be channeled into furthering ourselves mentally, physically, and financially. Just because we were handed a tough lot in life does not excuse us from trying to be better than we were before. The idea that you are bound to fail simply because society has robbed you of your rights is damaging. Correct that by recognizing what you have and channeling it for your greater good.

The Crippling Effects of Racism

Racial discrimination is something that people of color are intimately familiar with. It is a part of our daily experience. So, I am going to spare you the problems and focus on the areas that are related to the reasons you bought this book.

1. Negative Stress

Racial discrimination triggers stressors in our environment that make it difficult for us to truly live on terms that are favorable to us. Picture this; you are in the middle of a beautiful day. The weather is perfect, your co-workers are all on their best behavior, you are feeling fly in your favorite outfit...in fact, everything is going swimmingly well. And then suddenly, an angry white person calls you a dressed-up monkey. It doesn't matter how amazing your day was. Everything goes downhill from this point onwards. Your tongue starts to feel like a thousand needles are stuck into it, there is a sinking feeling in your stomach and your sweat glands start overcompensating. This is negative stress. It has a paralytic effect.

2. Self-Sacrifice

To survive this harsh climate, we have been forced to put other people's thoughts and opinions before and above our own. This kind of lifestyle has been so glorified that any thought of deviating is met with labels such as selfish or self-serving. The reason for accepting this way of life is to either form alliances that aid our survival or establish a safe environment for us to survive. In other words, we trade our identity so that we can have access to the most fundamental human right; the right to live. The racial profiling that is prevalent in society has caused many of us to sacrifice ourselves leading to distortion and dissatisfaction with who we are. When you are out of touch with your true self, your ability to reach your full potential is grossly limited.

3. Self-Reliance

This sounds like a good thing, and in some ways it really

is. But when it happens under our current social conditions, it can have a crippling effect on communal growth. Self-reliance entails depending on yourself. As humans, we all need to have this basic life coping skill. However, if it is borne out of an environment that generates deep mistrust in other people, it becomes a hindrance rather than a step in the developmental process. We are communal by nature. A few pages ago, I talked about how our formative years are defined by the community. You can thrive alone, but you need a tribe to truly enjoy life. Over-dependence on self can lead to mental and physical isolation. The shared community space becomes a poisonous well that keeps breeding distrust leading to some of the social ails that are evident in black communities today. This holds us back as individuals and as groups.

Finding Your Place in Society

Given everything we have learned so far, finding your place in society is key for the next step on your journey. And to do that, you must exercise some form of awareness. To know the problem is to solve it. If you have or are exhibiting any of the characteristics listed in this chapter, you have created awareness in part. You still need to do a lot of research and perhaps seek psychological counseling to help you understand why you act the way that you do. Just make sure that in your search, you don't work with people who either try to justify the unfair treatment you have experienced or minimize your pain. You have come too far to go back to the diet of lies and poor palliative measures drummed up by people who want to be heroes. Be aware of the truth, of who you are, of where you have come from, and the reasons behind each of these truths. Don't worry about where you are going. That is another step on this journey.

The next step is to accept the truth. Again, this is something I talked about earlier, and is a prerequisite for this part of the journey. Embracing the truth about who you are allows you to create pathways for the solution. The longer you deny the truth, the tighter the cycle that keeps you trapped to the point where the web of lies becomes your life. The truth is not always easy to accept. Sometimes, it is unpleasant. The idea that we are victims of a society that was supposed to help us become victors is not something that is easy to swallow especially when you lay that knowledge against the background of racism. That we missed out on several opportunities simply because of the color of our skin is enough to make any sane person boil with anger and resentment. But that is the truth, plain and simple. It doesn't mean that society is out to get you and ruin you. This is a system that has been in place for hundreds of years. Until the fabric that makes up society is changed, that is just the way the machine works.

However, you are not a machine. You are human. You are a woman, and you are black. That means a lot. Regardless of the psychological messaging you may have been fed, you have a place in society. You are important. You matter. Not just to the people who brought you into this world or who nurtured you, but to the world. Your role might be small, but without that void being filled up, the world would be 'less.' But with your presence and with you working in your power, the world becomes richer. It took a long time for me to get this message. I felt like I was too insignificant to matter to anyone. It was like if I vanished today, there was no one who really cared. This thought made me feel trapped. I didn't want to die because I was afraid of how isolated my death would be. But at the same time, living was tough because I still felt isolated.

Sometimes it feels that way especially when you are put in a competitive environment where it feels like everyone else is doing better than you. Imagine your legs tied up with a rock attached to it and then being forced to run a race (under threat of death) against people who are driving cars. Sounds impossible right? This is the reality for black women today. This is why it is remarkable that some of us even succeed at all. I believe that this speaks to the strength and magic of being a black woman. You need to key into this. If you continue to walk in the light of your truth and in the understanding of your worth, you will realize that you have a place. At the end of this book, you will also find your voice. For now, you are going to take things into the next chapter where we talk about finding purpose in who you are.

CHAPTER SIX

Expanding and Finding Purpose in Your Blackness

I used to be strongly offended when people started sentences with the phrase, 'you black people' or 'you black women.' It was almost as if somewhere along the line, I became a collective and my identity was irrelevant. But over time, I understood that I have prejudices of my own (we will get to that soon). I also learned to understand that people who phrased things like this were often prejudiced. They have a vague notion of what a particular set of people are supposed to look and act, and they impose this on everyone with similar features. Sometimes, their notions are based on prior experience, but they refuse to individualize that experience. Rather they use the lessons from that experience to characterize every person they meet. It is kinda like the same way people travel to one country in Africa, visit a specific locality, and declare that entire Africa is the same as the place they visited. It used to drive me crazy.

This was until I had a conversation with someone who I consider a mentor. According to her, when you have a negative experience, your brain subconsciously analyzes the environment and points out what it considers the key instruments for initiating that trauma. This becomes your trigger. So, whenever you are put in an environment where those key elements pop up together in a specific pattern that your brain interprets as dangerous, it triggers an alarm. When this behavior or thought process is repeated constantly, it becomes your truth. People have associated black culture with negative triggers. They see a man with long dreads and feel that he cannot be professional. They see a woman with a big, curvy body and analyze it to the point where the woman is sexualized against her will. Our music, dressing, and even the way we socialize have been given negative labels, making it difficult for us to freely associate with our blackness.

This chapter is about learning to take charge of that narrative. Changing people's perceptions of you is a task that will take a very long time. However, changing your perception of yourself is something you can start working on right now. Not only will it enhance your experience in life generally, but it will also help you embrace every aspect of who you are. It will help you find purpose in who you are. If you have been running away from yourself because of what other people think about you, this is the part where you stop, take a closer look, embrace it, and start believing in it. Your blackness should not be defined by society. You are the only one that should determine what being black means to you. You have been given the necessary tools to get started on that journey. The magic and strength that come with being black are already in your veins. Now is the time to use it to propel yourself forward and achieve your full potential.

The Truth About Being Black

Here is a simple assignment I want you to carry out. Get on your browser and search the phrase, 'black women are...' Leave it at that and then click search. Chances are your top 10 searches are going to contain negative commentaries about black women. I did it and my search results included conversations about how women are advancing in the marketplace, but women of color are lagging. There was also talk about how black women are victims of sexual assault, abuse, and so on. This is the image they have of you and me as black women; victims that can be taken advantage of. They don't tell you that one of the richest self-made women in America is a black woman. You don't get to see that kind of representation. Instead, they try to project what they want you to see in yourself. Thankfully, there is a way to combat these lies, and that is by using the truth.

Social activists use the word "representation" a lot, and there is a reason for that. When you see yourself reflected in a positive light in society, there is a ripple effect that trickles down to those in grassroot environments who may be stuck in tough conditions without hope. But when they see someone like them doing great, they can be inspired and be given hope/strength to push further. You need to start being more proactive when it comes to building or creating black women's representation in your life. Here is what I mean. Start by looking at a list of people who inspire you. Go over their track record. Let their proven success be a positive trigger in your mind. You will get a lot of negative news about an experience a black woman is having somewhere. Don't let that be your only representation in the media. For every negative message you get, replace it with a positive one.

Black women are doing amazing things, and they didn't start today. Whether in the field of science, activism, media, or religion, you will find powerful and influential black women who pioneered change during their time. The problem is not that black women are not present in these situations. It is the lack of reporting, or rather underreporting, that has undermined their efforts. While we wait for the world to get off their seats and do what is needed, it is our job to be proactive in searching out these women and giving them the credit that they deserve. This is not just for the people who are getting these accolades. It is also for us to validate our power, strength, and brilliance. But most importantly, it is to help pave the way for those who are coming after us so that they might look up and see the light that will lead them to their next destination. We must start teaching ourselves and the next generations that we are more than our circumstances. This is the truth about being black. We are more than our skin. We are bigger than our limitations and we are definitely not the people society paints us out to be.

Why Your Blackness Should Be Celebrated

The celebration I am talking about here is not the collective one we hear about like the holidays dedicated to our heroes. I am referring to the private celebrations. We know that there is black history month dedicated to educating and celebrating the history of black people. But celebrating your blackness is about acknowledging things about you that are linked to your roots. The way you talk, the texture of your hair, the color of your skin; all these things weave a biological story about where you come from, and you should celebrate it. History has not always favored black people because the people who wrote history were biased. However, you are the one in charge of your narrative. And yes, you may be biased toward yourself, but I will take that over destructive self-criticism any day. The point is you have a chance to rewrite your story. Are you going to focus on the scared black girl that everyone thinks you should be? or the strong black woman that you are?

Girl, you have survived extreme odds to get to this point. The fact that you are sitting with this book in your hands is a testament to what you have had to go through. Don't ever take your victories for granted no matter how little they are, especially on your quest to heal and find your confidence. You must learn to celebrate your wins. We think that until we hit those huge milestones in our lives, we haven't accomplished much. This kind of thinking will make you feel like a hamster on a wheel. You just push yourself and spin round and round for no absolute purpose. But when you enjoy each moment and savor every win, you empower yourself with confidence, making it easier for you to walk with your head held high because you are aware of who you are and what you have achieved. You know the doors you had to break down to create opportunities for yourself and you know that you are going to open doors for other black girls. This is worth celebrating.

Most importantly, you are going to celebrate your blackness because those things that people taunted you about have now become your most prized features. Some people say that black people dress funny. Well, that fashion sense is what you are going to celebrate today. Even if you don't dress the way society thinks black people should be dressing, it is still okay to celebrate and recognize it. This is a big part of where you are coming from, and is a part of who you are. Your strong black features like your nose, your eyes, your lips, and your body are things you are going to celebrate. It is time for you to take a bold step towards the mirror, look into it as you strip off all your clothes and tell yourself, "Damn, I am beautiful." Celebrate the color of your skin whether you are brown or black. Being a black woman means you come in different colors, shapes, and sizes. Celebrate this difference. Celebrate the ways that your body and features contribute to the diversity among black people. Celebrate your name. Whether it is the more 'acceptable' names or the ones that we are known to answer. This is who you are. There is no shying away from it. Embrace it and don't just embrace it. Celebrate it.

Gain Mastery Over Your Narrative

This last part of this chapter is a pivotal defining moment for you because until you take this step, the rest of the chapters in this book are going to be futile. It is time for you to take charge of your narrative. You must first learn to make peace with who you are. Whether you are big or skinny, whether you are a deep shade of black or a lighter shade of black, you must disassociate your sense of worth from these physical markers and then work towards accepting yourself as you are. Even if you intend to make changes in the future such as probably losing weight, the first step in that process is learning to love yourself. If you starve yourself of self-love because you feel you are now at a place where you think you should be, you create a template for the relationships you are going to have with other people because you are subconsciously sending the message that until you jump a certain hoop, you are not worthy to be loved.

For this reason, you must tell your story differently. You have heard a lot of things about yourself. Some of it has been positive. Some of it, negative. Now this is where you key into those positive reviews you have gotten about yourself and then tune out the negatives. Focus on positive feedback. Let that message stir up that good vibe inside you. Use the emotions that come from it to inspire a new list of positives. Let this become your affirmation. I am strong. I am beautiful. I am powerful. I am wise. These are just a few of the affirmations you can use to change your narrative. You are not what society says you are. I have said this several times in this book, but the reason I repeat it is that these false narratives have been repeated from the day you were born. And to counteract it, we must repeat the truth. You are your own person and that is perfectly okay.

At some point in this journey, you will experience a

broad range of emotions. You might start out with sadness before experiencing boiling rage. This is okay. Identify those emotions and acknowledge them. Let them stew up a little so that you can understand where your pain is coming from. The moment you get clarity, you should find a way to channel those emotions. Either through journaling, working out, or even just taking a nice long walk on a sunny day. I baked my feelings. Find what works for you. This will help you purge the negativity surrounding these emotions and help you see a brighter path. It is from this path that you can now begin the next phase of your journey.

In the next chapter and the chapters after it, our focus is going to be on you as an individual and as a woman. So, approaching that with a clear head and stable emotion is important. If you find yourself struggling to move on from the information you have absorbed in these past chapters, you might want to talk to someone about it. That is another thing we have to learn to embrace in our community - prioritizing mental health. It is part of changing the narrative. Your mind is just as important as your body. So, when you find yourself struggling mentally, don't hesitate to seek help. It doesn't make you weaker, and fighting your pain alone doesn't make you stronger. While we learn about our history, we will uncover the mistakes that people who came before us have made. We have paid the price by growing up under the consequences of their actions. However, we don't have to live with those consequences or let them determine our stories going forward. We can heal ourselves so that the impact can flow down to the people who come after us.

CHAPTER SEVEN

Identify Your Worth

The only person that can determine your worth is you. People will have an opinion of what they think you should be worth, but it will always be just that; their opinion. What stands out is what you say about yourself. In this chapter, our main objective is to help you determine your worth. In this context, we are not looking at what you should expect to be paid at your job or business. We are working on developing a strong idea of how you feel you deserve to be treated. Confidence comes from knowing who you are and what you are worth. You can walk into any room regardless of the atmosphere and still feel bold enough to be yourself while making the people in the room feel comfortable being around you. Knowing your worth is not undermining the worth of others to establish yours. It is having a keen sense of awareness.

Some people have built their confidence around breaking down the confidence of other people. This is a temporary fix and is only going to lead you to the path of bullies in society. True confidence comes from taking all the necessary steps and putting in the work and that is what we are going to try and do in this chapter. When you are trying to build your confidence after healing from trauma, one of the first things that goes out of the window is your sense of self-worth. Depending on what spectrum your personality lands on, whether you are narcissistic or reclusive, that worth could be overinflated or underestimated. Neither works well for your image, especially when you plan on working with other people.

Eventually, we will get to the part where you figure out how to deal with your personal struggles while working with other people. For now, we are trying to build a solid image for you from the inside out. This is an area where people usually make a grave mistake. They start by trying to build confidence from the outside in. Nothing wrong with that, but it doesn't last long. When you start the process from the inside, you build a solid foundation that can carry you through the toughest circumstances.

Confidence that relies on external factors is very superficial. Things like making your hair, getting new clothes, working on your body size, and so on are all external factors. I am not saying that it is not important. Of course, it plays a role. But if you don't work on the stuff that is inside, all that effort you put on the outside is going to be wasted. On that cheerful note, let us begin.

Who Are You?

As black women, our identity is hidden under layers of labels and social tags given to us by society. It is almost as if from the day we made our debut on earth, the rest of the world decided that we weren't good enough from the start. Our hair is meant to be styled a certain way to be presentable. Anything less is considered wild and untamed. They control our speech and our ability to procreate (the latter was done in some form). But no matter how much they try to silence us, that black girl sauce comes through on the other side making more people want to be like us. This is a clear demonstration of the fact that we have something inside of us that is worth emulating. The best part? This thing that we all share is unique to each of us. What sister girl A has is different from what sister girl B has and so forth.

You just need to find out what your own brand of black girl magic is. Remember, we are different, but we all bring something to the table. The next line of action is figuring out what your "it" factor is. To do this, silence those voices in your head that tell you who should be and who you shouldn't. Especially when those voices create conflict every time you make a simple decision. Voices that say things like girls are not supposed to do this, girls don't do that, and so on are only there to bring you down. They speak based on the repeated negative messages they have received for the most of their life. These voices don't know the real you. And as of right now, you don't know who you are either. So, if you wanted to get to know a person better, what would you do? Ask questions. Start with the simple stuff like the 'what' type of questions. What do you like? What is your favorite color? What inspires you? The list is endless, but keep at it.

After these types of questions, you move on to the 'why' questions. Why do you like cheese so much? Why do you prefer morning runs to nighttime workouts? These questions will help you probe deeper into your mind. The deeper you go, the more intimate knowledge you will uncover. Another way to get to know yourself better is to teach yourself to rely on your instincts. No matter how much programming we undergo, there is a biological language that your body never forgets and that is your instincts. The more you use your instincts, the more reliable it becomes until it is one of the more reliable voices in our heads. Your instincts will snitch on your partner when they start cheating on you. The same instincts alert you when something is off. And when you want an extra shot of confidence, guess what? Your instincts. In very simple terms, ask yourself questions, but don't question your judgment.

Raise Your Standards

We have already established the fact that you deserve the best in life. However, just because you deserve it doesn't mean you are going to get it. You still need to require it. The reason a lot of people disrespect you is because you have not made it a requirement for them. In the book, "Think like a man, Act like a woman," one of the common questions that people asked was why their men hadn't taken their relationship to the next level. The response that Steve Harvey gave was that the women in that position have not made it a requirement.

What does this have to do with anything we are talking about? Basically, if you want to enjoy the best of life, you need to raise your standard, and the standard is not limited to material things. Just because we talk about raising standards today doesn't mean that tomorrow you will be required to wear only designer outfits. I said it before, the outward stuff is superficial and can only take you so far. It is the stuff that goes on inside that we need to build on.

Raising your standard is determining within yourself to demand better treatment. When people talk down on you, you don't engage them or entertain them. You put them on ignore. This will let them know consciously and subconsciously that if they want your attention, they need to do better. When you tolerate behavior that does not elevate you or befit your status as a black queen, you open the door for all sorts of disrespect. This is not just from men. It could also be from your fellow women. And it is not limited to romantic relationships. It happens in workspaces and social spaces as well. There are people that carry themselves with such grace and dignity that before you approach them, you find yourself adjusting your outfit so that you are presentable. Those people have created a standard with their expression, their movement, and speech. You know that you have to do better if you want to say something to them much, less expect them to respond.

In raising our standards, we also need to learn to change the narrative. People have concluded that black women who have standards are either difficult or materialistic. The reason is one of two things; the women in question were either unable to communicate what they wanted to achieve at the end of the day or they misunderstood what raising their standard means. This is why I talked about the designer outfit. You must understand that raising your standard doesn't mean you automatically become difficult to work with. It means that you choose people who choose you. If people are going to be reasonable with you, then you are going to be reasonable with them. People should not present unruly behavior and expect you to negotiate under such circumstances. You may lose some social or financial benefits here and there simply because you choose to stick to your standards. But in the long run, it will pay off. Eventually, word goes around that this woman does not take it from anyone.

Improve Yourself

Raising your standard is not a one-way street where you

expect other people to treat you the way you want to be treated but release yourself from any responsibility in that process. You will also need to put in that work to help you elevate yourself to that level in your relationship. Here is what I mean, when you step into a work environment and you want the respect of the people on your team, you must mentally prepare yourself for the expectation that you are bringing something to the table. When you have nothing to offer, it is difficult for people to respect you. I know that this sounds unfair but that is the environment that we live in. The purpose of this book is not to help you create a fair and balanced world. It is the help you thrive in a world that is unfair and unbalanced. When you step into any environment, you have to come 'correct.' What do I mean? Whatever skill sets you to have on your resume must be twice as impressive. Never make the mistake of having a resume that is better than you are in person.

I am not saying that you should undersell yourself so that when you apply in person, you are better. I am saying you should improve yourself every single day. It is a lot of hard work, but this is the kind of hard work that pays off. Let say that you are in the tech field. Make sure that your fingers are on the pulse of everything related to the tech world. You don't need to be a master at everything but having more than basic knowledge of your field of expertise can make you a vital addition to any team in any organization. And when people see value in you, they automatically respect it. In the same way, your appearance speaks volumes about who you are as a person. As much as it is superficial, we cannot deny that we live in a superficial world. Most people judge a book by its cover because the simple truth is people are not that invested enough to want to flick past the cover of the book in other to get to the content unless they see a perfectly packaged cover that appeals to their visual senses.

Putting in the required work in developing available skills sets, learning valuable new things, and contributing to improve what you do is the internal work. Polishing your dress sense can provide a confidence boost and even give you access to a different crowd. Talk to a stylist if you are not sure about your current outfit combination. For the most part, your instinct will guide you in this department because you'll be drawn towards outfits that reflect your personality. This is key because no matter how dressed up you are, if it does not align with that inner personality, there is going to be a mix and match type of situation. It would be like putting gold on the snout of a pig. People can immediately sense when you are not authentic. Again, dressing in designer outfits from head to toe will not fix this. This is why you need to put all the ducks in a row so that by the time you're ready to put yourself out there, it all makes sense. Work on yourself internally and then progress to that outward expression of self. The combination of both would create a powerful black woman image that automatically commands the respect you deserve. Get this right and the next phase will be easier.

Our next chapter is going to focus on another core area that defines us as black women, and this is our friendships. Black women are known for their sister girls who uphold them during tough times and hype them up when their confidence is low. We have unique friendships that just bring joy to the heart whenever you witness it. But you have to be strategic in building those kinds of friendships and that is what we will be working on.

CHAPTER EIGHT

Build Your Circle

Show me your friends and I will tell you who you are. This is an old saying that rings true to this day. My mentor is fond of saying, 'your net worth is defined by your network.' Connect with the right kind of people and you will go very far in life. But if you link up with the wrong set of people, the only place you are going to be is down. We want to advance ourselves. At the start of every new year, this is our resolution; to be better than the person we were the previous year and that's fine. However, one key area we don't put the work into is our inner circle. These are the people you turn to when you have those tough questions you cannot answer yourself. These are the people who bring opportunities to your doorsteps. I remember attending a business seminar a long time ago. One of the speakers said something about us being 6 degrees away from the solution to our problems. This 6-degree stems from your inner circle.

In essence, you know a person who knows a person who might know the person that can get you what you are looking for. The relationships you establish that go on to form your inner circle require a special kind of treatment. This is not just about managing your peers. This is about how you are reflected in and by this group of people. These are not your 'yes men' or minions. Neither are they the ones who stamp out an idea every time you present it. They are the fire to your raw gold material. They will purge out those impurities and bring out the best in you and you will do the same thing for them. We all want those kinds of relationships. Girlfriends that we can call anytime, any day. Our ride or die bitches* as we like to say. So, in this chapter, we are going to explore what it takes to get these people into your inner circle as well as the important things you need to sort out when building your inner circle.

Your inner circle is going to consist of different types of people. In fact, I like to encourage diversity. You have that person who is a money person. You have a businessperson. There is a fun person, and your contribution to the group. When you bring this together, you have a dynamic energy that motivates whoever is in that circle to be whatever they want to be. The media likes to show female friendships filled with unnecessary squealing, backstabbing, and boyfriend stealing. To say that this is an insult is an understatement. Female friendships are more than what has played out in the media. A lot of people will have you believe that having female friendships could be to your detriment but in truth, if you want to progress to the next stage in your life, you need genuine female friendships.

Identify Your Support Unit

Life is not a bed of roses. There will always be ups and downs and all of us need someone to be there when we are going through the hard times. That is what your support unit is there for. When you are looking at qualities in friendship, it is not enough to have people who laugh with you when the going is good. You also need people who are ready to step up when you are in no shape to be there for yourself physically or mentally. A support unit is comprised of friends and family. Every black woman needs her tribe. They not only love you, but they also respect you. They want what is best for you. Your support unit is more than just the people you call in the middle of the night to swap stories with. They are the ones you call when you sense an opportunity that will favor them. They are also the people that you support. You have to understand that a support unit should never be a one-way street. With all of this in mind, let us look at how we can build our tribe.

1. Find Yourself

My mother is often fond of saying 'like begets like.' Essentially, we naturally gravitate towards people who are like us. If you are lost, insecure, and unsure about yourself, you will attract people who are in the same boat. And people like that will find it difficult to support you and be there for you the way you need them to. Your inner circle is meant to consist of people who rub you the right way. Christians say, "Iron sharpeneth iron." You can't use plastic to get the job done. The iron would destroy the plastic. Stone can sharpen iron, but the relationship is not mutually beneficial. However, when you find a situation where iron is doing the job, both parties will enjoy it. You have to find yourself.

Know who you are. Understand your values. You must determine what direction you want to take in life. When you put in the work to get this done you will naturally gravitate towards people who share the same principles and have more to offer you.

2. Be open

Many of us have developed a subconscious image of what we think an ideal friend or member of our tribe should look like. I don't know whether this is because of the media's influence. When we begin searching for people to take up spots in our inner circle, we use this image as the yardstick to measure who we think the ideal friend should be. When you do this, you miss out on opportunities to meet truly great people. People come to us in different shapes and sizes. Their personalities will be different as well. It is left for you to do the work by getting to know them. In the process of getting to know them, you will find yourself naturally pulled to some people because of the previous point I mentioned. The shared interest and similarities will be the bond that draws you to each other. However, your openness and acceptance of them the way they are will help foster that relationship and take it to the next stage. Leave the criticisms and judgment aside. Get to see them for who they are instead of who you think they should be. Understand them on a deeper level and then decide where you want to go with them. And this brings us to our next point.

3. Have a tribe for different purposes

You may be lucky enough to find one or two friends capable of meeting your needs in every way. Before you misconstrue things, here is what I mean when I say meeting your needs. When you want fun, they are down to have fun. If you suddenly crave traveling, they are up for it. If you are trying to set up a business, they will link you up. Whatever it is you are trying to pursue in life, these girls are there for you. However, if we are going to be realistic, some people are better suited for specific needs. When you are looking for fun, you need people who will support you in that venture. A business-minded friend who will always try to stop you from partaking in activities that bring the fun. It is not because they want to bring you down. The problem is, they don't share that value with you. This is why I mentioned keeping your mind open. When you are more receptive, you open yourself to more people who can serve your relationship in different capacities. It is also why understanding yourself is critical to the process because then you know what you want and can identify people who can help you get what you want.

Set Clear Boundaries

If you want to stay authentic and retain this new identity you are building for yourself, setting clear boundaries is important. People wrongfully assume that boundaries are meant to keep people out. In truth, it serves a dual purpose. It restricts unwanted movement that leads to invasion of space, and it also contains people within a specific space. I have used the word space a lot because it is an ingredient that helps foster relationships that we are not aware of. Did you know that you are not just your person? You also have a space. Have you ever wondered why you suddenly feel irritated when a stranger moves too close to you and acts too comfortable around you? They don't need to touch you or even say something to you, but that invasion of space automatically pulls your guard up. That is why we need clear boundaries. However, the boundaries are not limited to physical space, and include what you are willing to do, when you are willing to do it, and how you want to do it, and then communicating that to the people who need to know.

Whether you like it or not, we all have limitations when it comes to our mental, physical, and emotional strength. When you exert that strength 100% of the time, you end up being drained and losing the capacity to serve or be of use to anyone. A relationship that has no boundaries will leave you drained and exhausted. In such a situation, you lose your voice and your identity. After everything we have worked on so far, this is not a desirable outcome. So, what is the solution? To set boundaries of course, and here's how you are going to do it!

1. Learn to say no

This is the number one rule for any relationship. You can't be the yes person. When you are feeling exhausted or when you are just not in the mood, it is okay to say no. Another thing to understand is how to say no. You must teach yourself to say it in a way that communicates your decision without making the other party feel rejected. It is a delicate skill, but one that you will master over time with practice. For example, if your boss comes to your desk 5 minutes before closing time and asks you to stay longer for a work project, if you are not up to it or you already have plans, you can say no, state your reasons and its importance to you. At the same time, you could offer to make it up to them some other time, but make sure your message is passed across.

2. Communicate your needs

When setting boundaries, you can't just get up and dictate what you want. People need to understand not just what you want, but the reason why. When people understand why you want these boundaries set up, they are more likely to comply. But this communication is only relevant when it comes to people who form part of your inner circle. For acquaintances or people you meet randomly, you must establish your boundaries from the very beginning so they know that this is how they relate with you. An explanation is not always necessary for those types of relationships. For the people you are close to, communicate your boundaries with compassion and respect for their feelings. Don't focus on just what you want. Understand their needs and then work things out from there.

3. Apply healthy boundaries

When your boundary starts affecting a person's actions or invading their privacy, you are doing it wrong. When your boundaries make a person feel less appreciated, you are doing it wrong. Healthy boundaries focus on improving the relationship, not isolating one party. For example, if you happen to have friends who come from different religious backgrounds, a healthy boundary in that relationship includes avoiding making hurtful jokes about faith. This is particularly important if you guys haven't gotten to the point where you can freely discuss each other's religion. This way, you respect what they have and create an environment where they are also expected to respect what you have. Anything outside of this can lead to resentment and hurt feelings

Avoid Toxic Relationships

One thing that must never be entertained in your inner circle is toxicity. It creates an environment that chokes ideas, cripples confidence, and makes it difficult for you to fully express yourself. Your inner circle is the one place where you can be yourself without fear of judgment. When you invite a toxic person into that circle, they bring the very things you are trying to get rid of. Some toxic people have masked their toxicity under the label of "concern for your well-being." They make it seem as though their harsh treatment of you can be justified by their so-called concern for your well-being. They are masters at gaslighting and making it seem as though you are crazy for questioning their words and actions.

A toxic relationship is a brand of trauma enabler that can mess with your psyche for years. That is because there is a bond that is forged in that relationship, an investment that is made into that relationship, and some level of commitment. You cannot easily separate yourself from this person. The image that comes to mind when I think of toxic relationships is securing chains around your neck and then attaching those chains to the horse that drags you on rough ground. That is how bad toxic relationships are. Unfortunately, it is not always easy to spot toxic relationships. Yes, there is physical and verbal abuse (which some women still struggle with extricating themselves from). But beyond that, spotting it can take time and during that time, you suffer greatly. So here are some ways to tell that you are in a toxic relationship:

Constant stress or unhappiness

I told you before that there are no negative emotions, and this is mostly because the emotions we like to qualify as negative are a natural response to things that are not favoring you. When you find yourself constantly stressed or unhappy, especially when those emotions are linked to a specific person, it is safe to say that you are in a toxic situation. Every relationship undergoes periods of stress and struggle. But when that period becomes prolonged or your happiness is far and few in between, you might be in a relationship that is cutting you off from your happiness. When you make this discovery, wallowing in the stress or unhappiness is not going to help. Your next step should be to find out why you feel that way and determine if the relationship is worth it. If it is not, have an open conversation with that person, express your feelings and see what happens.

You feel ignored

Black women have constantly had to deal with situations where someone is supposedly good to them with the expectation that they return this goodness with loyalty. I have had friends who were in not-so-great relationships but felt they had to stay there only because their partners were taking care of them. When you talk about this with regular folks, they focus on things like "he takes care of your bills, he makes sure you have everything you need, what else could you want?" What people fail to understand and thankfully there's been a lot of awareness created about it, is that we all have our unique love languages. There are specific things that people have to do to communicate to you that you are loved and respected. They can give you the entire world but if they fail to do these things, you are going to feel ignored and unappreciated. It's even worse when you have communicated this to them several times and they insist on doing things their own way. You deserve to be heard. You deserve to be respected. You deserve to be loved. Anything less does not serve you.

You keep hoping for change

When the relationship you are in is too focused on what will happen in the future rather than what is happening at the moment, you might be in a toxic situation. Let me explain. Perhaps you are with someone who you have had a lot of good days with, and you have seen what they are when things are going good for them. But over the years, they have become this unrecognizable person that doesn't do those things anymore. Still, you hang on because you are hoping that they will revert to what they were before or evolve into something better. Somehow, you have made yourself an anchor from this future you are hoping for. You are convinced that if you leave, things are going to take a turn for the worse. Maybe they told you that. All these suppositions are just indications that you are not in the present. One major reason we avoid the present is that we are unhappy in it and when you are unhappy, it's a sign that that relationship is toxic. Toxic doesn't have to mean abuse. It could be that you are in an environment that stops you from growing.

Family is not always a choice in the sense that we are born to who we are born to. We don't choose them. But you see your inner circle? They are the ones you choose, which mean you have the power to create the supportive community you are looking for. It is going to take time and it is going to take a lot of hard work. Most importantly, it is going to require you to step up to be the kind of person you want to attract into your circle. So be diligent about it. If you already have people like that in your life, work on nurturing those relationships so they can be what you need them to be. With a supportive group standing behind you, you now have twice the resources and energy you need to tune out those negative voices that have been implanted in you by society. That is our next step on this journey.

CHAPTER NINE

Tune Out the Voices

Everyone has a past. This past comes with moments of happiness, moments of sadness, and moments that we wish we could hide away from the rest of the world forever. But one fundamental principle of this book is owning up to your truth. Hiding your past is not going to make it go away or disappear. I have a favorite workout program that I like to listen to on YouTube. In it, one of the motivators says, 'you are already in pain, why not turn that pain into profit?' That phrase always gets me through my workout regimen no matter how grueling it is. I think it is just effective in this situation. You see, your past has already happened even though it was not ideal. It may be ugly. It may contain some of your least proud moments. However, rather than wallow in the events of something that has already happened, this is your opportunity to turn that past into the platform that will launch you into your future. Sounds impossible? Well, that is exactly what we are going to do in this chapter.

We are going to confront the memories you have of your past. Both the ones that fill you with pain and regret and the ones that keep you trapped in the glorious old days. It is time for you to move forward into this amazing life you were destined for. But to do that, you must properly handle your history. Remember, you are taking charge of your narrative. This includes going back to where it all started, reframing the story (not rewriting it) so that you can grab the lessons and the blessings, and then use them as tools to push you forward. I don't know what kind of life you have had but as a black woman, I am willing to bet that it wasn't exactly a smooth sailing one. Your past being crappy does not justify your inability to have a future that is bright and excellent. You have the power in your hand and as you come into the knowledge of who you are, you must equip yourself with the skills to turn that past around.

Before we go digging around your past trauma, you need to brace yourself mentally because you may find some information that may trigger emotions you may not be ready to deal with yet. You need to hit all the right notes with this. Try as much as possible not to get sucked into the emotions triggered by the trip down memory lane. Focus on the steps you are taking, not the ones you have already taken. Limit the judgmental attitude and try to be extra kind to yourself. If things start to get a little too difficult, remind yourself that you are a queen, you are boss, and you have everything under control. Plus, the past has no power over your present unless you hand it over.

Reframe Your Failures

Nobody likes to fail. The main reason we dislike failure is that we attach our identity to our failures. We feel that failing at something automatically makes us failures. Before we start talking about our personal failures, I want to point out that most of the people we look up to and consider extremely successful are people who have a lot of failures under their belts. There is no billionaire, CEO, or inventor who got to where they are without failing. And if you talk to them about their failures, one common thread you would find among all of them is the fact that they credit their success to their failures.

Surprisingly, despite this amount of history staring at us in the face, we still look at failure as a roadblock. Hopefully, we are going to change that in this segment. At the end of this, I want you to be able to look at your failures and say yes, I did that. That is how you reframe your failures. But there is more to it.

1. Retrace your steps

When you fall or you miss your way, the first thing you do is retrace your steps. This helps you figure out what you may have missed or what might have gone wrong. Retracing yourself is not for you to relive the failures. It is a logical way of analyzing how far you have come and what you would need to do to get over this barrier. Analyzing the cycle of failure and retracing your steps can be frustrating, but there is a lesson to be learnt. Every great inventor and great invention are a result of someone failing but not giving up. Instead, they analyzed their failures, retracing their steps until they got to the success point. We all have a success point and sometimes the failure we are running away from is what would take us to that success point. This is why giving up should not be your instinctive response every time you fail. Retrace your step, figure out what went wrong, and stay the course. It doesn't matter if the failure was in your marriage, relationship, business, or career, retracing your steps is always effective in helping you figure out the next step.

2. Forgive yourself

If your actions are not replicable but have changed your life, you need to forgive yourself after you have retraced your steps and figured out where you went wrong. You need to take responsibility for what you have done, or at least recognize your role in it. This is called accountability. It is a way of taking back your power especially if the mistakes you made trigger a lot of emotions, not just in you but in the people involved. Taking back your power may sound conceited, but it is essential if you are going to learn the lessons/blessings of any failure. Failure has a way of casting doubt over your abilities. It makes you question your every action. By taking ownership of your role in that situation, you regain a bit of your lost confidence. You then need to make the effort to forgive yourself. We are usually harder on ourselves than we are on others. Correct that and make forgiveness your priority.

3. Move on

Out of all the steps involved here, I think this one is the hardest. The concept of moving on makes it sound like you are a coward or you don't care about what has happened. I don't know where we got that ideology from. Still, moving on is the final stage in getting over a failure. When you fall, don't sit there moping over it. Get up and dust yourself off. If there is a cut, clean it and dress the wound. That is what we are supposed to do every time we experience failure. You take the steps that we talked about before and then you move on. If it is a situation that requires you to try again, do so. If it was an error in judgment, forgive yourself. If there is an opportunity to make amends, do so. And that is the essence of reframing failures. Don't lie to yourself about what happened, and don't chain yourself to the past either. Learn from it and move on.

Take Control of Your Fears

Only a fool or someone with a medical condition can say they are not afraid. Fear is a human response. It is perfectly fine to be afraid. The problem begins when you permit your fear to control you. As black women, we have so much to be afraid for and afraid of. However, we can't allow those fears to take over our decision-making process. It doesn't mean we shouldn't be cautious or apply wisdom in our dealings. But fear should not dictate our choices. There are countries where it is advisable not to travel alone as a woman. We hear a lot of horror stories. Does it mean you should cut out travel experiences completely? Of course not. For every unsafe city, there are dozens more that are safe. For every opportunity that might compromise your safety and overall life experience, there are even more opportunities for you to take advantage of. The only criteria are for you to gather the courage to step up to the plate.

Another thing you should know is that sometimes the fear we experience is second-hand. It is handed to us by either our environment or through the content we consume. I am a huge fan of crime shows. They fascinate me, but there is a downside to watching crime shows. It slowly erodes your trust in people. If someone makes a wrong move, your brain automatically interprets it as a possible influence that could cause harm or danger to you. This doesn't mean that you shouldn't take your fears seriously. Something is causing you to be concerned. Obviously, addressing those concerns will put your mind at ease but the objective here is to make sure that you are always in control. Even when you are thrust into situations that take away your control, it should not completely control how you react. The keyword in that sentence is 'react' because our reactions determine our experiences and our experiences influence the bulk of the message we feed ourselves.

When confidence is low, leaning back on your experiences can help create an environment that boosts your confidence especially if you have positive experiences. However, if those experiences are clouded by fear, it would only cause your confidence to sink even lower. So how do you combat fear in a manner that is significant and impactful? The first thing I will ask you to do is to grab your journal and write down a list of things that you would want to do. Right next to that list, write down what has stopped you from doing those things. The next step is to figure out how you can overcome those fears. The easiest path to a solution for that is to face your fears head-on. In other words, if you have a fear of bugs, set up a meet and greet. Doesn't sound exciting but after you have confronted the worst, its impact or influence over you becomes significantly reduced. The more you do it the less afraid you become.

Apply this to everything on your list and you find that the only thing that has been stopping you all this while was you.

Affirm Your Strengths

When you have multiple voices in your head telling you what you can or cannot do, making a decision in the midst of that chaos becomes difficult. The worst part is that it is almost impossible to feel authentic in that environment because of the conflicting messages, which in turn ruins your confidence. You have reframed your failures and worked on picking yourself up after you have admitted your mistakes, your next step is to silence those voices or at least turn them down so that you can hear yourself think. From my experience, the most efficient way to clean out negativity is to affirm positivity. In this case, the positivity we are going to affirm is your strength. If you are not a sports fan, I am sorry because the next analogy I am going to use relates to sports.

When you watch the players on the pitch, there are people on the sidelines waving, swinging their arms, and cheering. I am not talking about the fans. I am talking about the cheerleaders. No matter how rough the game is going for their team, the cheerleaders always chant the right thing. That is what affirming your strengths does to you. However, affirmations take things a step further. They create a bubble around your confidence that cushions you from the effect of the negative voices trying to bring you down. They also create an environment that enables your sense of self-esteem to grow. Affirmations put you in a positive light by allowing you to see the best in yourself even at your worst. Affirmations are a proactive way for you to reprogram your mind. After all that negative messaging, you are way overdue for the good stuff. So how do you affirm your strengths?

1. Accept yourself

Since we started this book, you have heard phrases like, own your truth, leave your truth, be yourself, and so on. All of this serves one purpose; to help you accept yourself the way you are. Now, accepting yourself the way you are doesn't necessarily mean you don't make any room for change or growth. It is simply setting up yourself to be the recipient of unconditional love. The kind where your love is not based on what you can or cannot accomplish. It is rooted in just being you.

2. Believe in yourself

Before you start saying your affirmations, you must start believing in yourself. The thing is, you can speak all the right affirmations from now until you are blue in the face, but if you don't have any faith in yourself and in your ability to be the best version of yourself, those words will not have any impact. Because I understand how much of a struggle this is, we are going to talk about it in subsequent chapters.

3. Compile a list

Write down the most amazing qualities that you have as well as qualities that you would like to have whether in your work area, finances, or in a relationship. Now phrase those qualities in a way that reflects your expected present circumstance. For example, if you want to be more confident, try writing an affirmation like, *I am a confident woman*. It is that simple. However, if you feel that you are struggling, you could buy a book of affirmations centered around the kind of topics you are interested in and highlight the ones that resonate with you.

After you have done all three things, you need to consistently speak your affirmations. It is that consistency that will ensure the message is internalized. If you miss a day or two, don't beat yourself over it. Simply get back into the game and continue like you never left. But if you find yourself distracted from your affirmations and the steps you are trying to take to get rid of those negative voices, it might be time for you to reassess your priorities and that is where we are going next.

CHAPTER TEN

Reassess Your Priorities

You are whatever you devote your time and efforts to. This is a message I have carried with me since I was a child. If I spend more than 70% of my time on social media, whatever content I absorb during that time will influence my thoughts and opinions. This is the part of your journey where you start putting everything you have learned about yourself into practice. When you know your interests, the things that you like, and the things that inspire you, it makes more sense to prioritize them over things that society expects you to handle. Also, reassessing your priorities is not about only focusing on the things that bring you joy. You are going to look at the life you are currently living and how it reflects your new identity. Like the relationships you have with people, do they reflect the respect and companionship you seek?

The health habits that you have right now, do they reflect the respect you have for your body? These are just the simple questions you will need to ask yourself in this part of your journey. Reassessing your priorities is not about turning your life upside down. It is just turning your attention to little things that matter to you so that you know where to apply effort for maximum results. The idea is to get yourself to a point where you are no longer active participants in the rat race. Instead, you enjoy each moment and live life to the fullest. You want to be a powerful black woman who is loved and respected. You don't do that by sticking to the things that people expect from you. If you follow that pathway, you might end up getting the power and the respect, but you'll also end up being miserable in your own life.

Misery and confidence do not work well together. One will amplify the other leading to even more misery and possibly fake confidence. There is something called imposter syndrome. This happens when you feel as though you are not qualified to have the life you currently have and one of its root causes is inauthenticity. This is usually because you are participating in things that don't represent you favorably. These range from the opinions of other people to keeping up appearances. This creates a toxic environment, and you already know how toxicity negatively affects confidence.

Stop Living For Others

Black women are experts at putting their life on hold to make other people happy. And I get it. We are communal people and when you are in a community sometimes you need to put the needs of a community over your own. But the thing with us black women is that we make it a lifestyle. We sacrifice for our parents and sacrifice for our siblings. When we get married, our husbands and children become the beneficiaries of our sacrifices. This life of sacrifice deprives you of an opportunity to live a rich and authentic life. If you are going to find your voice, what purpose will it serve if you fail to use it? You can't continue to live your life for other people. There must be a balance. This balance is where you cater to your needs and then manage the relationships that you have as well. Proper relationship management will ensure that your life is not built on the expectations of other people. We do this all the time and we don't even realize how much it affects us until it gets too late. But that is not the worst of it.

If the ball stopped with us, it wouldn't be a big deal. However, the sad reality is that we transfer this same cycle to our children. We expect them to live for us after years of sacrificing for their well-being. We feel that our reward as parents should be their sacrifices for us. We equate their love for us with their ability to cast aside their hopes, dreams, and aspirations in favor of ours. There is this joke about a mother and daughter preparing for the daughter's wedding. The mother took charge of the wedding and the daughter complained about it. The mother's response was this, 'when I was getting married, it was my mother's wedding. Now that you are getting married, it is my wedding.' This pattern of behavior hurts us, especially us black women. Living to please other people is not really living at all. To truly live is to get to the end of the line and be able to say yes, I live up to my potential. But how can you say that when you don't even put yourself in a position where you can take advantage of opportunities?

It is like we operate on a system of debt. You are made to feel indebted to other people for your existence and therefore you must pay these people. This payment can mean that your choice of study in school is determined by other people. Where you work can also be determined by other people. This is so wrong. I am not even going to touch the illusion we have built around ourselves when it comes to social media relationships. That would need a whole new book on its own. But that behavior didn't start with social media. It started in our own homes and that is where the fixing needs to start. We need to learn to put ourselves first. It sounds selfish but the truth is, when you can serve yourself, you create an emotional environment that enables you to become even better at serving other people. One thing I want you to remember from this segment is that as black women, we hold the key to the growth of our community. If we thrive, our community will thrive. If we find happiness, our community will do the same. So, by being selfish and focusing on yourself, you can unlock that life that allows you to become a better advocate/ambassador for your community.

Set Your Own Expectations

When I set up my first office, my friends gifted me with wall art with the inscription, 'be your own boss.' It was a very simple phrase, but it made me feel empowered. I decided my work and play hours. I handle 100% of the risks and 100% rewards. It was everything I wanted. But certain people ruined it for me with their snide comments. They would make little jokes about my 'small' business or how the 'little lady' was trying to make her way in a big world. They said they meant well but I could hear the sarcasm dripping in their voices. It is not like they intentionally wanted to put me down i. These people had expectations for, me and I was not meeting them. After many conversations over the background of mixed emotions, I found out that these people fell into two categories. The first group felt that I had too much potential to be wasting it on a small business and the second group didn't expect me to get this far.

What I learned from that experience is that no matter what you do, you can never completely satisfy people. You are damned if you do and damned if you don't. People will always have varying opinions and expectations. There is nothing you can do about that. But jumping the hoops and making yourself less just to satisfy those expectations will slow you down and make it impossible for you to focus on your wants and needs. Sometimes, we don't even realize what we are doing. We want to be daddy's perfect little girls, so we bend over backward even when it brings us pain. To get the approval of mommy dearest, we make compromises that hurt us in the long run. In extreme cases, we treat those expectations like oxygen. Without them, we feel empty and lost. I have heard people claim to find their purpose in these expectations. This kind of attitude is not limited to family members. You have heard of the label 'a teacher's pet.' Kids with that title are eager people pleasers, and it doesn't get better as they grow older.

If you are one of those kids, it is time to stop the circus. You can't be wasting this beautiful gift of life by waiting on other people. Healing mentally and emotionally requires making important life changes. It may not be comfortable to make those choices, but the reward is more satisfying than the initial discomfort. Girl, you can't fully kickstart your journey under the weight of the expectations of other people. They are only going to block out the sunlight and limit the joy you should be experiencing. You are a daughter of the earth. Our skin was made to glisten in the sun (literally and figuratively). That is the reason for that melanin magic. Get out from under that cloud and step into the light. And speaking of clouds, we have one more to get rid of.

Let Go of Past Regrets

Living with regrets is like driving a car with your focus on the rearview mirror. It distracts you from the journey ahead and keeps you stuck in the past that you no longer have access to. Because your focus is not where it should be, you miss out on important moments in your life. But that is not the only thing you will miss out on. There are opportunities, pleasure, and leisure activities waiting for you to experience them every day. Being preoccupied with regrets caused by past actions or inaction will either blind you to these experiences or make you hesitant about taking those leaps. So, why are you being held back by regrets? And what can you do going forward? Well, that is what we are about to find out.

Feelings of regret are not isolated events. We all experience it on some level. On the surface, it is not entirely bad. When you are trying to reframe past failures, regret can be an excellent guide as you retrace your steps. However, things start to get a little tricky when you revisit the past and instead of accepting things for what they are, you paint alternative scenarios with different outcomes. This can make you feel good temporarily, but you are not confronting the real problem. Without the truth, you are like a dog chasing your tail around in circles. You are essentially trapped in a cycle. When you are stuck, moving forward is not always easy. But it is not impossible.

For starters, stop focusing on what you could have done differently. Confront that past, face the truth (the role you played in it), learn the lessons you need, and then face forward. This sounds easy, but these are a lot of steps you need to take. Depending on your regrets, one of those steps might include making amends to the people you wronged. Another important step is forgiving yourself. Beating yourself over an incident that happened in the past won't do anything except drag your confidence down. And girl we are way past that at this point. Wondering how to move forward? Make up your mind to do so and just do it. Stop waiting for some grand sign or event to happen. Just do it. You know that there is so much out there waiting for you. Grab the proverbial bull by the horns and get ready for the ride.

CHAPTER ELEVEN

Reclaim Your Excellence

Do you know why we struggle with our confidence? That is because somewhere along the line, we forgot how awesome we are. We allowed self-doubt, other people's negative opinions, and expectations to crush our esteem. We permitted negativity into our space and let it become a domineering thought or voice in our head. When you forget who you are, it becomes easy to buy into the narrative other people are selling. We have said a lot of things up to this point. We have talked about the problems we encounter as black women. We explored our pain, opened ourselves to our passion, and I think that is enough for now. I want to introduce you to someone you may not have met before. Or maybe you have, but I think a reintroduction might help.

This person is the definition of the word beautiful. Her beauty radiates from within and shines through to the outside. When she walks, her movements are those of a powerful goddess. When she speaks, grace and elegance flow through her words. She is strong and fierce, and at the same time, she is delicate and flexible. She is wise and patient. She is kind and eloquent. She is aware and smart. She is everything she needs to be for herself and more. She almost sounds too good to be true, but that is our girl. She is a woman of excellence in every sense of the word. I am pretty sure that you already have an idea of who this woman is, but just in case, let us hear those drumrolls please…the woman is you.

How do you feel about being this woman? If your first reaction was disbelief, it is okay. Anyone would feel intimidated in the presence of such a person and the idea of comparing yourself to them? That is a lot. So, I understand the disbelief. But after you are done with the segments in this chapter, that will change. If your reaction on the other hand was excitement, congratulations girl. You are a rock star, and you know it. The rest of this chapter is going to help you embrace that message. Reclaiming your excellence is how you reposition yourself to receive all the great things coming your way.

Believe in Yourself

If you are going to become the best version of yourself, you need a team of one; you. Of course, you have your tribe backing you, but this one-man-army is going to get you started. You need to be your own cheerleader, fan, and believer. It is nice to have other people do this for you but if you can't do it for yourself, their efforts will be like trying to store water in a woven basket. Useless. Well, not entirely useless, but definitely not enough to get you through long-term situations. So, let me walk you through the 3 members of your army. Let us start with your cheerleader.

This is the second inference I am making to this preppy group of people who seem to be perpetually happy. But it is for a good reason. Life will always toss the storms your way now and then. Being your own cheerleader teaches you the ability to find healthier ways to cope when things get too tough. Rather than seeking validation in places that cultivate an unhealthy mental environment, you look inward and fortify yourself against the negative voices that want to creep in. As your cheerleader, chants like, *you've got this,* or *you can do this* should be your mantra every time you are confronted with impossible situations.

Right next to our cheerleader is your fan. You have to love your work girl and I don't mean to love it from the perspective of a person enjoying what they do. I mean having great appreciation and value for your work. Have you seen the beehive go crazy over Beyonce's work? You don't need to go that crazy, but they could be excellent pointers when it comes to how to be a fan. One thing about fans though, no matter how crazy they are, they never accept mediocrity. The goal is excellence and when it is achieved, they celebrate it. You should do the same. This brings us to the last point - you must believe that you are enough. Never compare yourself with anyone else. And if the doubts start creeping in, take things back to the cheerleader. You can do this!

Unlock Your Passions

What does excellence mean to you? Best of the best at your job? Making great sales? Generating good reviews for your brand? I think it is about adding value. Black excellence doesn't only celebrate what society considers the best and brightest. It is about the people who elevate our community through their valued contributions which are not always monetary. When you look at the people we celebrate, they come from all walks of life but there is a common thread, they are all doing what they are passionate about.

Excellence is not about who rakes in the biggest buck or who has the fame. Excellence is about contributing value. You could be working your boring desk job and still be adding value in your own way. But when we put your confidence on the table, you have to consider other options. Following your passion is one of those options. You get the chance to use your skill or talent in a way that makes you happy while adding value to society. Passion is an important ingredient in your work because when you hit a roadblock that makes you consider quitting, it (passion) will get you over that bump.

We have only one life to live. Wouldn't it be better to spend it doing things that bring us joy while providing value to society at the same time? There is so much going on in the world. So much pain. So much sadness. We can't fix it for everyone. Neither can we make everyone happy. The only people whose happiness we are completely responsible for is ours. Instead of spending each day stuck in routines that bore you and provide you with zero inspiration, why not take up things that give you joy. Your passions do not need to have monetary value, contrary to what social media motivators tell you. It should simply give you joy and value.

Dream Big Dreams

If you want to make your way in this life, you are going to hear a lot of nos before you get to the yeses. When someone says yes to your idea, it is the most refreshing thing in the world. You feel empowered. You feel loved and appreciated. But the no can be soul-crushing. If you are not mentally prepared for it, your confidence levels will tank, and it feels as though you have lost your ability to dream. No creates a vacuum in your heart for fear to roam freely. And when fear roams, you become overly cautious. You stop yourself from taking a leap because you are afraid of getting shut down again. You don't stop dreaming but you stop yourself from dreaming. A life without dreams is a life without hope. And girl, if you are going to reclaim your excellence, you need to start dreaming again. And not the safe, small dreams that keep you in your comfort zone. You need to dream big.

Dreaming big can be scary. Mostly because you are filled with the overwhelming thought of how you are going to make that dream come true or if you are capable of getting it done. This is understandable, but it is also a classic indication of fear. From my experience, fear of dreaming arises from the loss of control. You feel that you don't control all the factors needed to make those dreams a reality and because there is no control, you feel everything else will fall apart like dominoes. But you must understand that dreams are not valuable because of your ability to make them come true. They serve a higher purpose.

Dreams are a non-risky way of expanding the world around you. There are no limitations when it comes to your dream. You can be a zookeeper in Madagascar. A ballerina in France. An all-star athlete in America or even a bad-ass Bond girl in Britain. My point is, there are zero restrictions. Given that our reality consists of social rules and standards that keep us caged in, this is an excellent avenue to explore what life's alternatives are available. Think of dreams as a gap year that you can take any time you want. No consequences. No responsibilities. Just explorations. If you focus on the right dream, you feel motivated and excited to follow your passions. When you meet a black girl who has those kinds of dreams, you better believe that she can do anything. And with that, we make our move to the final chapter.

CHAPTER TWELVE

Take Care of Yourself

Self-care is you prioritizing your needs. As black women, we have been raised to put everyone else before us. We have rooted our identity in self-sacrifice so much that we feel like we are not serving if we are not sacrificing. We sacrifice our peace, sanity, and physical health for the people we love. I have met ladies who suffered domestic abuse in their relationships. They had the ridiculous notion that the abuse was an expression of love. To reciprocate that love, they felt they had to endure the pain and torture. Even in other relationships, we put ourselves at the receiving end of pain, and worse, we normalize it.

This has to stop. Another behavior I have noticed that is common among black women is the damsel in distress syndrome where we suffer in silence as we secretly wait for someone to rescue us. But at the same time, we put up a facade of strength even when we need to be and feel vulnerable. This need to present a front while hiding away our true feelings relegates us to the bottom of the list in our own lives. It is unhealthy and contributes to our inability to feel confident in who we are. Throughout this book, we have explored the various ways we can get back on our respective thrones and reclaim our crowns. We have talked about the tough stuff. Now, it is time to talk about the easy stuff.

Our focus in this chapter is nurturing our minds and body. Looking after our overall health can give us the much-needed confidence boost. When you are healthy, you feel good about yourself. You feel more competent when it comes to pursuing your goals and going after the life you want. Caring for yourself gives you permission to feel good about yourself. It is a way of communicating to your mind and body that you are invested and committed to your wellbeing and emotional growth. When it comes to investments, no type of investment can pay off like investing in yourself. I did say you are your biggest asset. Taking care of yourself will ensure that you remain in prime condition for longer. Now, let us look at the three main ways you can care for yourself.

Nutrition

I used the word nutrition here instead of diet for a specific reason. We often equate diet with nutrition when they mean two different things. Nutrition refers to getting the most from your diet. It is not about hitting a bodyweight goal or following the latest health trends. It is ensuring that your body gets everything it needs to stay healthy. Beyond that, it focuses on teaching you how to have a healthy relationship with food. As women, we are more prone to stuffing ourselves with food as a way of coping with our emotions. If I were to get a dollar every time I sat on my couch and cried my feelings into a tub of ice cream, I would be able to afford a month-long vacation in the Caribbean. While this happened occasionally for me, for some women, it is a standard routine. Whenever you feel sad, you eat. Feeling anxious? A nice chocolate cake can fix that. I must admit, when you are doing it, it feels really good. Even if its only for a short time, we still do it anyway.

When you do this, you are not giving your body the nutrition it needs. You are simply covering up the problems under layers of junk food that could pose a health risk for you in the future. Not to mention how the food impacts your body which in turn affects your confidence. On the flip side of eating junk food is focusing on specific food groups because of their purported benefits. Internet diet experts declare some foods as superfoods and highlight their benefits. People who buy into the benefits refuse to include anything outside those foods in their diet. The problem with this is that those benefits become temporary because there is no balance in their diet.

Proteins are great for bodybuilding, but you still need key nutrients from all the other food groups in order to make the most of your diet. Unless you work with a certified nutritionist in developing your diet, you may not be getting the most from your food and this might be having a negative impact on your health physically and mentally. Don't be too eager to get on any diet no matter how much hype it gets on social media. There have also been studies that link certain foods to elevated moods. And I mean the kind of mood elevators that won't impact your waistline negatively. The key to enjoying food is balance and portion control.

Rest

In today's world, a hardworking woman is someone who works 3 jobs and barely gets enough time to sleep. In the media, the ideal modern woman is seen dashing off to her office with coffee in her hands looking frazzled and constantly running out of time. Black women taking vacations and living a less frantic lifestyle are considered baby girls or sponsored girls. This image of black women needs to be changed. The overworked black woman is an image that has been glorified for too long and that needs to end.

Taking time to rest is not slacking off. It is you valuing yourself and your contribution to the team enough to give yourself time to recover. If you have read the biblical version of the creation story, you would know even God rested on the 7th day. We like to use the term 'super woman' a lot. It is a great compliment. To be compared to a fictional woman who possesses superhuman strength feels good, but it forces you to try and mimic her strength, which includes working round the clock. The truth is a lot simpler. You are human and you need rest the same way you need oxygen and food. A person who has gone a long time without rest experiences a significant reduction in their ability to perform. The bottom line? Rest is recommended and you shouldn't wait until you are completely exhausted to get it.

Part of your self-care routine should be rest. Rest doesn't mean laying down in your bed and sleeping. Treating yourself to a day at a spa or nail salon is a way to schedule some time for yourself. Meeting your girls later in the day for happy hour is another way to let off some steam. The goal is to let your hair down, relax, and unwind. I love to see black girls getting spoilt, especially if they are doing it on their own dime. Plan your vacation months ahead. Pick a cool location preferably somewhere with a perfect view of the ocean. If that is too far off into the future, grab a few buddies and go hiking. Taking a walk in nature is said to be very therapeutic. For us creative folks, it connects us to our creative muses, giving us much-needed inspiration to improve our respective art forms.

Counseling

Black people like to think that the mental health crisis is white people problem. This is a joke that we share to downplay our mental struggles. We buy into the social narrative that we are strong mentally and physically and therefore our minds cannot be influenced or twisted by the struggles we face. But the truth is, we have dealt with so much trauma that it would take a miracle for any black person to succeed or even exist without combating one form of mental health issue or other. Our men are constantly under scrutiny because of the prevalent racial biases, and this puts them at risk of going to jail or getting killed by the people employed to protect them.

The same racial biases prevent us from having access to much-needed health care facilities in our communities, leaving us dealing with preventable debilitating health challenges. Our women face different forms of abuse every single day. This creates the perfect environment for mental health issues to thrive. We need to stop trying too hard to be strong and focus more on trying to heal. To heal, we must first accept our biggest problem, which is the mental health struggle. We have a lot of negative misconceptions about mental health issues that when a person is struggling with mental health, we believe they are broken and weak. Because of this, we refuse to associate ourselves with anything related to it even when we are confronted with the truth.

We are more open to fixing our problems with pills and surgical procedures. But sometimes, our problems are more psychological than physiological, meaning that the treatment lies in talking to a specialist. It is only from there we can develop the solution that will bring about healing. Remember what I said earlier about how the success of one black woman can influence our community and bring about the success of that community? One black woman who was put in the work to heal from her trauma can instigate the same chain of action in her community and this is a great thing. We need to open ourselves to the idea of counseling. We can't expect to forge healthy relationships with people if we are still carrying the baggage of our past. In addition to all the narratives we need to change, eliminating the stigma surrounding mental health issues and their treatment would serve our community a lot.

If we put down this baggage, it will help us find ourselves, and in so doing we find our passion. And through passion, we find purpose. It is only through that purpose that we can create the type of value that will help build our community, which is the end goal. Counseling requires you to admit that there is a problem. Arriving at that conclusion takes courage and I believe you have what it takes. You are brave. You are strong and you have survived things that your peers will probably never be able to imagine. But you are also human and to fully survive your trauma, you need to heal. It is time we open up and start talking to the experts, and that I believe is the final step in this journey. You have done all the work and will continue to do the work but to take things to the next stage, you need to talk to someone.

Conclusion

Finally, we have come to the end of this book. In the process of writing this book, I had to revisit a lot of old wounds, and this took its toll on me emotionally. I can only imagine the journey that it took you on. It probably hurts. Here is the thing about pain; it is indicative of the problem. The pain you feel tells you that there is a problem and more importantly, it tells you that you are on the right track. You have boldly met your pain head-on. Don't stop now. You owe it to yourself to get to the finish line. The end of the book is simply the beginning of another chapter. What that means is entirely up to you.

Perhaps it is the chapter in your life where you diligently apply everything you have learned so far to improve your quality of life or you open a new chapter in another book so that you can build on the foundation that this book has already laid. And these are just two of many options. I hope that you realize that life is waiting for you to come out of your shell and live it. Unfortunately, time is ticking by. Each precious moment is only as valuable as we make it. It is time to make it count.

Know that when you make those queen moves, you are not only doing it for yourself. You are doing it for the little black girls who are watching. You want them to know that there is so much they can achieve if they set their minds to it. You are also doing it for the ladies who came before us. You want them to know that their efforts, struggles, and sacrifices were never in vain. They walked so that we can run. We must break those unhealthy cycles and build a new way of life for ourselves. You are the hero you have been waiting for to rescue you. Step up to the task with courage and confidence. Silence any voice that attempts to diminish your power.

I am so excited about this journey. I know that you will do great things and I look forward to hearing your story. Until then, keep shining and keep winning.

Thank You

Before you go, I just wanted to say thank you for purchasing my book.

There are many books on the same topic, but you took a chance and chose this one.

So, thank you for choosing me and for reading this book all the way to the end.

Now, I wanted to ask you for a small favor. **Could you please consider posting a review for the book? Reviews are the easiest way to support an independent author like me.**

Your feedback will help me continue to create books that will help you achieve the results you want. So, if you enjoyed it, please let me know.

Thank You

Made in the USA
Monee, IL
25 September 2023

43423358R00089